DESIGNING THE BEST SELF

BUILDING BLOCKS FOR A BRILLIANT LIFE

Hooma Roy Choudhury

INDIA • SINGAPORE • MALAYSIA

ISBN
Hardcase 979-8-89322-772-7
Paperback 979-8-89277-576-2

Author's page - www.hoomaroychoudhury.com

Dedication

I dedicate this book to God, the embodiment of the highest wisdom and to all my gurus.

May this book find a place in your life where you know that better outcomes in life result out of balance and our continuous efforts towards improving ourselves - learning how to use the body, breath, and mind (the building blocks) as tools to our own advantage.

CONTENTS

FOREWORD

This book delves deep into the three fundamental questions of human existence as to how we function, what drives us, and why we do what we do. The book aims to provide answers and insights into the mysteries of human nature and offers practical guidance on how to make the best out of this life. From the enigmatic depths of our emotions to the complex interplay of our thoughts, the human experience is a journey through a labyrinth of questions, a quest for understanding that has captivated minds for centuries. I hope this book becomes a transformative experience, offering not just answers but also the tools to shape a life that resonates with authenticity and meaning. As we navigate the enigma of our existence, may these insights serve as a companion, guiding us towards the discovery of our true selves and the realization of our fullest potential.

Part 1

Introduction

1.1 LETTER TO MY READERS

Dear friends,

I decided to write this book because I believe we all need some guidance on how to make the best out of our lives while facing all sorts of situations, without bringing any religion, caste, creed, or parent/ grandparent into the picture. In a world teeming with challenges and uncertainties, the quest for a meaningful and purposeful existence becomes increasingly vital.

The outcome of life largely depends on the choices and decisions we make. Our attitude is our choice, taking action or not is a choice, and the way we look at any event is our choice. And the same choices we make, both big and small, determine the path we take in life and ultimately shape our future as a result of that.

But how equipped we are to make the right decisions or make the right choices depends on many factors and is not limited to just time or age. It depends on the knowledge shared by our previous generations, on our surroundings, our exposure, the memory accumulated over past years and lifetimes; and then conscience (Buddhi) - the awareness level based on learnings.

If that is the case, obviously there will be different choices and different outcomes for different situations. While we don't have control over all factors, there is one factor - knowledge shared among generations - where there is a scope of influence for better outcomes and better handling of situations.

We all know that there is a huge amount of dependency on parents/ grandparents as the first gurus. What we do with our human lives/ how we face situations/ what we become, partially depends on how evolved our previous generations were.

This seems unfair, right? Because if parents didn't know how to take care of their physical and mental health, they may not be in a position to teach the right things to the next generation and would not be able to give us the right path of guidance or advice. There are chances that they can set wrong examples and teach the next generation unhealthy ways of leading their lives which can result in making/taking bad choices.

This incorrect or half-baked knowledge can continue to be passed on from one generation to another and, in most cases, people would learn and make changes in their knowledge bank through their own experiences (either painful or divine in the case of yogic lives.)

So, is there a way we can streamline or summarize a few basics on human life which are tried and tested over years into one guidebook that each one of us can use, including children? Just as we study basics of mathematics or science, shouldn't there be a common basic knowledge guide or manual on human life that each parent/grandparent must read and share with the next generation? An easy one for the modern world so that we know how to better prepare ourselves for life.

I believe, there should be a simple standard guidebook on our human construct, our nature, our rights and duties, and how to operate optimally in this human life for each one of us. And we must gain this knowledge as early in life as possible.

What if we could correct things from the start itself? In fact, such knowledge is a precious gift to be given to anyone, starting with couples planning their family, parents, to be parents, teenagers & more. We should give it at nursing homes, maternity centres because one of the biggest jobs that we do is to bring up and nurture a human life- our own life as well the life that we give birth to or bring up.

We all want to make better choices, we all want better outcomes, right? We all want to feel empowered & equipped to deal with our toughest situations.

And so, here is my sincere attempt to present the required Knowledge in one of the simplest forms. I have not created this knowledge; rather I would say that I have acquired it from life lessons and which has always existed over the years in various forms in various books or research works. The intention is to present it in a simple form, relevant to present times, and make it a standard based on the evidence of its usefulness.

Yes, I have learnt the hard way and my learning after failing and falling still continues. I wish there was a course on how to handle ourselves in the school itself. In fact, I personally feel that it would have been better if the course was part of my parent's education and we would have learnt things by default.

Hope this effort proves fruitful in your life. Wishing you all health, happiness and abundance at all times. This book is for everyone, starting from a to-be-parent to a-parent to children & teenagers who can read. One happy child will one day become one happy parent. And one is a million, enough to bring the change across.

Please note - I do not have the authority to preach or guide, am only writing and presenting what people with authority on the subjects have said before. Personally, I have applied the tools given in this book to survive my most difficult life situations and have also seen remarkable results. The choice to accept or reject the knowledge and the tools completely lies with you.

1.2 MY BELIEFS AND PHILOSOPHY

We are a small unit of God. We have life; we have energy, and we have the power to create. But we may or may not be best at doing our job due to our level of awareness (which differs from one to another) and freedom to choose basis that.

In order to get better at our jobs/ get better at choosing, get better at facing life situations, and get better at creating, we need the ability to see and understand the entire picture (increased level of awareness and knowledge).

Taking an example here, as I remember the story of the elephant and the blind men. It goes like this…

Once a king called one of his men and said: "Assemble all the men in the kingdom who were born blind together in one place" Having done as the king commanded, the king then said to the man, "Now show the blind men an elephant." The man did as the king asked him to do.

This having been done the king addressed the blind men saying, "Have you seen an elephant?" and they replied, "We have sire." "And what is an elephant like?" he asked.

And the one who had touched the head said, "An elephant is like a pot." while the one who had touched the ear said, "An elephant is like a fan."

The one who had touched the tusk said, "An elephant is like a spear" while the one who had touched the trunk said, "It is like a snake."

The one who had touched the body said, "It is like a wall," and

the one who had touched the leg said, "It is like a tree." The one who had touched the back said, "It is like a mortar", the one who had touched the tail said, "It is like a rope" while the one who had touched the end of the tail said, "An elephant is like a broom."

I would bring a twist to this story. Let's say that the men are not blind but they can understand only the part that is in their syllabus or that is in front of them felt with their senses.

I would also name the men now.

First man is Mr Science who only believes in the hypothesis proven till date. It has enough evidence for the elephant's trunk so believes in the trunk part only.

Second man is Mr Religion, who only goes by what's his interpretation of the holy book is. As per him, the book says an elephant is big like a wall, one has to bow down. So Mr. religion believes that and always bows down.

Third man is Mr. Experience. He only goes by what he saw, heard, or felt. He could only touch the ears in this lifetime, so knows about ears only.

Fourth man is Mr. Media. Gets largely influenced by what the majority says. Most people said an elephant is like a snake, so for Mr. Media, elephant is like a snake and hence is already scared to touch it.

The Fifth man is a suave, well-read person who is logical and goes by who is saying what? He believes more on the credentials of the author than on his own exploration. His understanding of the Indian elephant was largely influenced by a British author who came to India for 2 months to study elephants and had enough citations to prove his theory about elephants. As per the Britisher, the Indian elephant is a mythical character and feels like a fan. So, our well-read person believes an elephant is a fan.

So on and so forth.

Who do you think can understand who an elephant is, to decide/ choose any action basis that?

Most of us are in similar situations, touching only one of the parts of the whole and interpreting ourselves and the world with our little understanding.

Accepting that we are not seeing the whole is a good point to start, which means we are open to possibilities and not concluding about ourselves & others or everything else around. It also means being open to learning.

The immediate next step then is to prepare ourselves physically, mentally, emotionally to learn and gain more understanding and awareness.

An empowering journey starts with curiosity, improving awareness level and gaining more understanding. As we gain more knowledge and awareness in life, we start choosing our response instead of reacting in a default mode. Our choices determine the way life unfolds.

If this sounds very difficult to digest or, if you are someone who is thinking, ' everyone knows this obvious thing', let me assure you that in the following pages of this book while I take you through a step-by-step approach, and give you the tools of empowerment, you would realize that every complex creation (within or outside) has a simple and obvious base. We only need to go back to the basics.

Part 2

Basics of Human Life–Body, Breath & Mind

The question is why? Why we need to know about ourselves (human construct)? We can simply take birth and continue to inhale and exhale as long as possible and then die one day. What's the need to know anything else?

Firstly, because we are part of nature (this creation or existence) so we are nature too, hence, we are governed by the laws of nature or existence. And we need to understand, acknowledge, and abide by the same laws of creation or nature before anything else for a peaceful co-existence.

For instance, say if you decide to stay in a new house in a new locality. You would do a minimum of two things to start with - Check the house properly where you wish to stay, collect all information about it, check the details of what you need for your stay there and then check the locality & your surroundings too.

Assuming it's a wooden house, you would be especially careful with fire elements to be able to live and maintain it.

And, suppose it's a quiet locality. You know you would also have to maintain the same. If your family is loud and ends up fighting every other day, you can't stay in such a locality for long. Others will object, revolt or, even throw you out.

The house here is our body that we stay in and the locality here is our world/our surroundings/our environment around us.

We stay in the body – We need to understand the body and its nature

We use the mind – We need to understand the mind to use it to our advantage

We stay in this world – We need to understand our relationship with the world

We need to know the rules of the game to play better. It's as simple as that.

The more aligned we get with the laws of nature (existence or creation), the better would be the balance within as well outside in the world. Otherwise, we know what happens when there is imbalance within us or outside in our environment.

If you don't believe that laws of nature govern us and everything around us, from the smallest particles to the largest being, let's see a few examples

Gravity: One of the most fundamental laws of nature, gravity, governs the motion of objects in the universe and determines how they interact with each other. Whatever we do, we must follow this law of nature.

Thermodynamics: This law states that energy cannot be created or destroyed, only transferred, or converted from one form to another. We are governed by this law which is evident in the way that our bodies use energy from food to power our cells and sustain our lives.

Evolution: The theory of evolution also is based on the idea that all living things are governed by the laws of nature. It explains how we adapt in response to environmental pressures, and how natural selection determines which traits are passed on to future generations.

Ecology: The laws of ecology govern the relationships between organisms and their environment. They determine the availability of resources, the distribution of species, and the impact of human activities on the natural world. If we go against it, we have to face the repercussions.

Genetics: This governs the inheritance of traits and the transmission of genetic information from one generation to the next, which shapes the diversity and characteristics of different species including humans.

Secondly, we all want to be healthy & happy as humans. And since we don't have direct control over many things outside of us, we need to start with ourselves and do at least our part well. Which means making the best use of what we have - Body, breath and mind.

Well, hopefully you would agree that the first gift we get when we are born into human life is this body, breath and mind. This is what we have with us and in our sphere of influence. Everything else comes after that.

However, as soon as we arrive in this world, we start to learn about other things including our society & media depending on the exposure.

Education on how to use mind, body, and breath properly in our lifetime is not something that happens deliberately or as part of the norm. We take all this for granted

Unless we know what to do with our body, breath and mind, how to use these properly, how can we expect better outcomes?

It's like going to the cricket ground with an intention to perform well, without knowing how to use the bat.

Point is, if we can operate ourselves better as a human life, outcomes can be better not just for ourselves but for everyone else around. And as it goes, one happy (balanced) life would lead to one happy home, one happy home would lead to one happy (balanced) world.

The keyword here is balance, internal as well as external. For simplicity's sake balance means no extremes.

Any extreme is imbalance when behaviours or actions are exhibited to an excessive degree.

Examples

- Workaholism - Neglecting health, family and relationships for the sake of profession/professional goals.
- Irritation - In the same traffic on the same road one person may drive peacefully enjoying the music while the other may get bogged down on the road and shout at everyone. This is imbalance.
- All diseases from thyroid to diabetes are a sign of imbalance - Imbalance in nature, actions and in body.
- Abuse of any form - Language to physical.
- Either pampering the child beyond a limit or beating the child.
- Exaggeration of speech, Overselling anything, or social isolation on the other hand.
- Excessive exercise and no rest.
- Passion at times can lead to imbalance when other things are neglected including duty.
- Extreme highs and lows as a result of substance abuse.

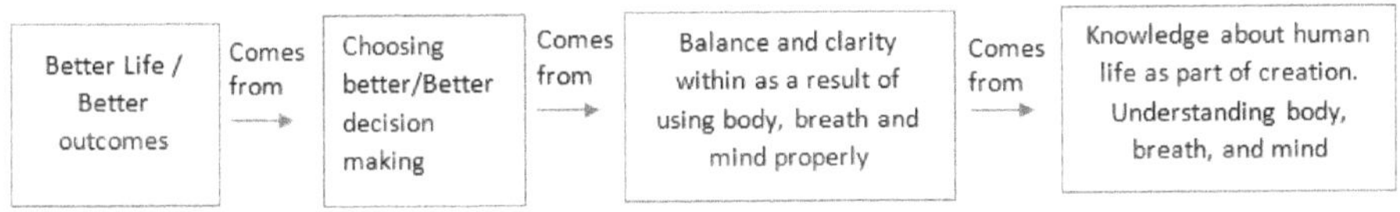

Who wouldn't want to move from pain to pleasure, from chaos to direction, and from ignorance to evolution? Besides, what option do we have other than to learn and learn with the least resistance?

Whether you pick up any mythical story or take examples from natural disasters, or look at physical health as criteria, we know whenever anyone has acted blind and failed to align to the laws of existence, ruin or destruction has followed.

We are talking about life. Human life. For how long can we continue to play blind? In fact, growth and evolution are inevitable and applies universally to all aspects of existence, encompassing not only physical transformation but also non-physical development. This fundamental truth underscores the essence of life itself—an ongoing journey of change and progress. It is a reminder that every entity, from the smallest microorganisms to the most complex organisms, is bound by the intrinsic force of evolution.

Creation doesn't give anyone the privilege of staying the same and not growing or changing. The dynamic essence of existence propels individuals, societies, and even ideas forward, fostering a continuous process of growth and change. Just as a seed transforms into a flourishing plant, individuals undergo personal development, adapting to new experiences, acquiring knowledge, and evolving in their understanding of the world.

Sometimes the change is drastic, sometimes it is so slow that we forget to acknowledge that in the short term, but change is bound to happen any which ways. Embracing change becomes a vital component of the human experience, fostering resilience, adaptability, and the ability to thrive in a world that is in constant flux.

Now, how do we choose to learn, grow & change which makes all the difference - by pain or by insight or awareness?

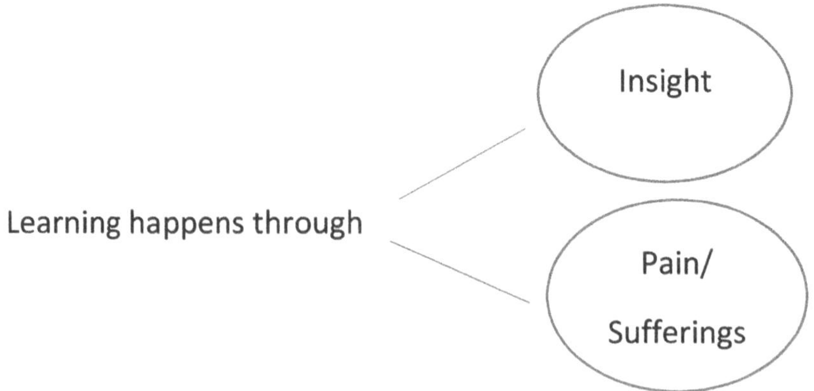

Insight (improved awareness) leads to predictive intelligence that is good judgement of future consequences. When the judgement is good, the choice of action in the present is good. Insight comes when there is balance and clarity.

Do you know many of the well-known inventions, discoveries and significant breakthroughs have resulted out of insight even when the problem at hand seemed insurmountable.

1. Isaac Newton's theory of gravity: According to legend, Newton was sitting under an apple tree when he saw an apple fall to the ground. This observation led him to develop the theory of gravity, which explains why objects are attracted to each other and fall to the ground.
2. Einstein's theory of relativity: Einstein had a breakthrough insight in 1905 when he realized that the speed of light was constant, regardless of the observer's motion. This realization led him to develop his theory of special relativity, which transformed our understanding of space and time.
3. The discovery of the double helix structure of DNA: James Watson and Francis Crick famously had a moment of insight while working on the structure of DNA. They realized that the structure of the molecule had to be a double helix, which allowed them to solve the structure of DNA and revolutionize our understanding of genetics.
4. The periodic table of elements: Russian chemist Dmitri Mendeleev is said to have dreamt of a table in which all the elements were arranged in order of atomic weight. When he woke up, he quickly jotted down the details of his dream, which led to the development of the periodic table of elements that is still used by chemists today.

5. The structure of benzene: In the late 19th century, German chemist Friedrich August Kekulé was struggling to understand the structure of benzene, a molecule with six carbon atoms and six hydrogen atoms. According to legend, he fell asleep by the fireplace and had a dream in which he saw a snake biting its own tail, forming a circle. This inspired him to propose that the carbon atoms in benzene formed a ring structure, which was later confirmed by experiments.
6. Archimedes' principle: In ancient Greece, Archimedes was tasked with determining whether a crown was made of pure gold or had been adulterated with other metals. While taking a bath, he noticed that the water level rose as he entered the tub, which inspired him to use water displacement to measure the volume of the crown and determine its purity.
7. The invention of the telephone: Alexander Graham Bell famously had an insight while working on a project to transmit multiple telegraph messages over a single wire. He realized that he could use the same principle to transmit speech, leading to the invention of the telephone.
8. Leonardo da Vinci's inventions: Da Vinci had many insights and moments of inspiration that allowed him to create some of the most innovative and revolutionary inventions of his time, including flying machines, armored vehicles, and a submarine. His insights were based on his keen observation of the natural world and his ability to imagine new possibilities.
9. The sewing machine: In the early 19th century, Elias Howe was struggling to invent a machine that could sew at high speeds. According to legend, he had a dream in which he was being attacked by a group of warriors with spears. In the dream,

he noticed that the spears had small holes near the tip, which inspired him to invent the eye-pointed needle that allowed the sewing machine to work efficiently.

10. The melody of "Yesterday" by The Beatles: Paul McCartney has claimed that the melody for the song "Yesterday" came to him in a dream. He woke up with the melody in his head and quickly wrote down the notes before he forgot them.

Learning through Pain is opening the eyes and changing the course of actions only after suffering. This is the result of poor judgment of future consequences. For e.g. - One decides to change only after falling sick, or losing near and dear ones because of wrong habits or company. There is no dearth of examples where humanity has learned big and obvious lessons only after going through suffering

The recent one being Covid. From the value of time to not taking heath or relationships for granted were a few lessons among many that covid taught us Here's are a few famous examples when learning has happened through pain.

1. The Holocaust: The atrocities of the Holocaust were a painful and tragic experience for millions of people. It taught us significant lessons about the dangers of racism, prejudice, and genocide. The painful experiences of Holocaust survivors and witnesses have contributed to a better understanding of the need for tolerance, empathy, and respect for human dignity.
2. The civil rights movement: The lesson on the need for greater equality and justice for all came only after civil rights in the United States which involved many painful and difficult experiences, including violent attacks, arrests, and discrimination

3. Renaissance: The painful experiences of war, disease, and political instability contributed to a renewed interest in classical learning, humanism, and the pursuit of knowledge, which led to some of the most significant cultural achievements in history during renaissance.
4. The discovery of penicillin: Alexander Fleming's discovery of penicillin was the result of a painful infection that nearly cost him his life. After observing the growth of mold on a contaminated petri dish, Fleming realized that the mold was producing a substance that was killing bacteria. This insight led to the development of penicillin, which revolutionized the treatment of bacterial infections.
5. The discovery of anaesthesia: For much of human history, surgery was an excruciatingly painful and dangerous procedure. However, only through a series of painful experiments and trials, medical pioneers like Crawford Long, William Morton, and Horace Wells discovered and developed the use of anaesthesia, which allowed patients to undergo surgery without feeling pain.
6. The story of Steve Jobs at Apple: Steve Jobs was famously fired from his own company, Apple, in 1985 after a power struggle with the board of directors. This painful experience taught Jobs the importance of humility, collaboration, and the need to build a strong team. When he returned to Apple in 1997, Jobs restructured the company, focused on innovation and design, and built a culture that valued creativity, teamwork, and customer satisfaction.
7. The story of Ford Motor Company: In the late 1990s, Ford Motor Company was facing significant financial challenges,

including declining sales and profits. One painful decision that the company made was to sell its successful luxury brand, Aston Martin, to raise much-needed cash. However, this painful experience taught the company the importance of focusing on its core brands and products, and helped Ford restructure and streamline its operations.

8. The story of PepsiCo: In the 1990s, PepsiCo faced intense competition from Coca-Cola and other beverage companies, and struggled to maintain its market share. One painful experience for the company was the failure of its Crystal Pepsi product, which was marketed as a clear cola but failed to gain traction with consumers. However, through this pain, PepsiCo learned important lessons about product innovation, market research, and the need to stay true to its core brand values.

9. The story of Airbnb: In the early days of Airbnb, the company faced many challenges, including regulatory hurdles, safety concerns, and the need to build a reliable and trustworthy platform. One painful experience for the company was a series of negative press stories about guests who had trashed their hosts' homes, which threatened to undermine the company's reputation and credibility. However, through this pain, Airbnb learned important lessons about the importance of trust, transparency, and user experience, and developed new policies and procedures to address these issues.

10. The story of Steve Waugh: Steve Waugh is one of Australia's most successful cricketers, known for his gritty determination and leadership skills. However, early in his career, Waugh struggled to find his place in the Australian team and was

dropped several times. One painful experience for Waugh was being dropped from the team for the 1993 Ashes series. However, through this pain, Waugh learned important lessons about resilience, mental toughness, and the need to work hard to improve his game. He went on to become one of Australia's most successful captains and batsmen.

11. The story of Netflix: In the early days of Netflix, the company faced many challenges, including competition from Blockbuster and the difficulty of scaling its business model. One painful experience for the company was the decision to split its DVD-by-mail and streaming services in 2011, which resulted in a loss of customers and a plummeting stock price. However, through this pain, Netflix learned important lessons about

12 The story of James Anderson: James Anderson is one of England's greatest bowlers, known for his swing and seam bowling skills. However, early in his career, Anderson struggled with inconsistency and injuries, and was dropped from the team several times. One painful experience for Anderson was the 2006/07 Ashes series, where he was dropped after a series of poor performances. However, through this pain, Anderson learned important lessons about the need to work hard on his fitness, technique, and mental approach. He went on to become one of England's most successful and

Insight vs pain is like prevention vs. cure.

So, let's learn about basics of human life, about our nature - our mind, body and breath.

As they say, 'Awareness prevents and dissolves suffering'

2.1 OUR BODY

Yes, we all know we have 206 bones, more than 600 muscles, around 78 organs. The smallest unit in our body is a cell. Cells form tissues, tissues form organs, organs form organ system and organ system form an organism including a human body.

Cells -> Tissues -> Organs -> Organ System -> Organism

Interestingly, the average adult has somewhere 30–40 trillion cells, and an estimated 242 billion new cells are produced every day. Try writing this number 242 billion new cells to understand how much change we go through on an everyday basis without realizing that most of the time.

For the whole body of a human being to function, each of these cells needs to do its job. Who is telling them to do their job? Brain? Huh! The brain, too, is made of cells. Who is telling the brain cells to do their job then?

There has to be inbuilt intelligence in our system, right? Intelligence in each of these cells.

From cells to a full human system, there is intelligent programming done by the creation so that our bodies can function well. Now the way software programs get viruses, our body and cell intelligence also get impacted by the inputs we feed into our system.

The process of inputs impacting intelligence starts from a mother's womb and goes on forever. So, we get the culprit now- inputs that we feed into our intelligent system.

If inputs support the inbuilt intelligence, we would have healthy, balanced lives. If not, then we would see from birth defects to diseases to complete shut-down physical as well as mental. The outside world is just a reflection of what's inside us, so let's talk about balancing one life at a time.

What are the inputs that impact our body?

Food, water, air, thoughts including memories (good or bad) that we keep saving in our system. Every day 242 billion new cells apart from the existing ones are impacted by the inputs fed to each of our cells. Imagine!

The good part is we have the option to rebuild ourselves every day in the way we want just by being conscious of the inputs that we feed ourselves.

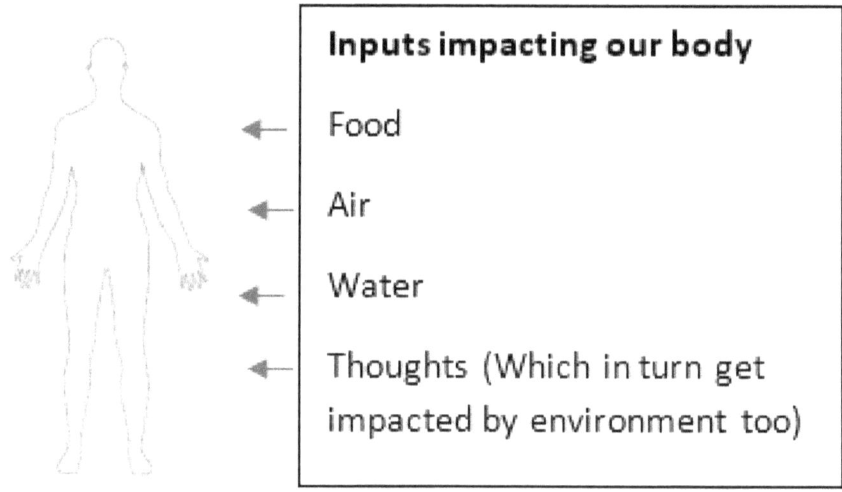

2.1a Food

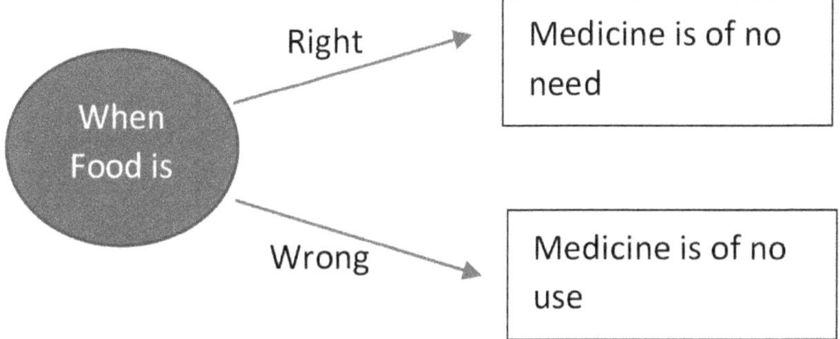

Whatever we eat becomes part of us. Thumb rule to eat right is to listen to our whole body, not just the tongue. Food is meant to give us energy. If at all it makes us lazy, sleepy, agitated and ill in any way, it can't be the right food even if it is the so-called home cooked food by mom.

In fact, a lot of unhealthy eating habits start at home. Force feeding children, asking them to eat fast, and then sweets, chocolates and pizza being offered as rewards at home. Most health issues come from what we eat and how we eat. Indigested and stuck food in our system causes most health issues.

Let's learn about one of the most important inputs to our system:

What to eat: There are the basic food principles that come straight from scriptures - The Bhagavad Gita & The Essene Gospel of Peace (Reference -Sattvic movement)

- **Food should be living food** – should have prana (life energy). If something is cooked on fire, we must eat it within 3 hours, a maximum of 5 hours. We should eat Living Food that comes from Mother Nature, not something that is lying in the fridge after being cooked days ago or manufactured or processed months ago. Avoid ready-to-eat manufactured or processed products. At home, one at least knows when the food was made, what all things were used to make, how it was made, and in which utensil it was made.

One has no idea of the prana present in the food at hotels and restaurants. They handle so many orders, most of them use pre-mixed ingredients. Besides, no one can say with confidence if the ingredients are truly organic or inorganic, the served food is 2 days old or 1-day-old, if frozen ingredients are used to prepare or farm fresh. Which utensils are used to cook - Teflon coated non-stick cookware, microwave or aluminium… no one knows.

If frozen food is taken out, fried and presented immediately, we consider it freshly prepared, right? So please know and acknowledge all this. Learn to cook so that you can understand the ingredients that go into your favourite dishes and how good or bad they are for you and your case. Extremism is not needed even when it comes to eating out, but being aware and choosing balance can help. Remember, each individual is different, and accordingly, each body is different. Individual has to be treated as a whole for food to become a medicine and not poison.

- **Food should be wholesome** – We need proteins, carbs, vitamins and minerals. Mother nature provides each food item with a specific ratio of carbs, protein, fats, nutrients–so that we humans can digest and eliminate it with ease. However, when we process the same food that comes from nature & eliminate or subtract certain things and modify that, our bodies can't digest that well. Hence, trust the intelligence of mother nature and eat most foods exactly as it exists in nature as far as possible.

The simplest example is bread or naan made with refined wheat flour- Maida. Refined flour is made by removing the bran and the germ from the wheat grain. This procedure removes numerous essential nutrients present in whole wheat flour along with the fiber. As a result, consuming refined flour (Maida) solely contributes to calories and swiftly raises blood sugar levels, similar to consuming table sugar. These blood sugar spikes lead to feelings of sluggishness and prompt hunger shortly after consumption. This way, we consume more calories than we would otherwise. Besides, food without enough fibre sticks to our intestines for long and you know what happens if you leave food for long. It rots.

- **Food should have rich water content** – We have 70% water within us, so obviously our food has to be alkaline and rich in water content to maintain the same ratio because food becomes part of us every time it goes in.

  Water-rich content foods are raw fruits and vegetables- Apples, oranges, avocados, mangoes, carrots, broccoli, olives, spinach, bananas, tomatoes, etc.

- **Food should be plant based** – Whatever one can eat in raw form exactly as it exists is the natural food. Humans can eat fruits and vegetables in raw form, so that's the food meant for us. Carnivores can eat meat in raw form, so that's meant for them. Their digestive systems are such that they can digest it. We humans don't have sharp nails and teeth to tear animal meat apart. We don't have shorter intestines, like animals or strong hydrochloric acid. The food stays for long in our digestive canals before getting eliminated, so we should be eating what stays fresh for long. Imagine what happens when you leave meat outside for long compared to fruits and vegetables. Raw fruits and vegetables have a longer life than raw meat or, for that matter even cooked meat.

You may ask why are we talking all the above? Because we need healthy gut which results from healthy growth of good bacteria. Good bacteria, often referred to as probiotics, are beneficial microorganisms that help maintain a healthy balance in the gut. They aid in digestion, nutrient absorption, and support the immune system. We need to feed our good bacteria through every meal that we take. And our good bacteria need complex carbs and fiber to survive.

Consuming probiotic-rich foods like yogurt, kefir, and fermented vegetables can help promote the growth of beneficial bacteria, while avoiding excessive intake of sugary, processed foods and antibiotics can help prevent the proliferation of harmful bacteria.

Healthy gut means high energy and calm mind which is what we need to make better decisions.

Points to remember: Eating right is necessary but much more important thing is eliminating the wrong. You also eat fruits, you also have vegan milk, you also have salads is not enough if you do that alongside 80% of your meal containing fatty, fibreless carbs rich or sugary foods.

70-75% of each meal has to be right and relevant to your case. Also, the number of times you eat right is important and it should be 95% of the times at least. Now, if you travel 50% of times in a month or year, and say I eat cakes only when I travel. It would be unfair. It's no longer a once in a while thing then. So, take care. Honesty is your choice.

Balanced diet: This is something we have all heard from doctors to nutritionists to science teachers. Every science book showed us pictures of balanced meals, explaining that we need protein, minerals, vitamins, carbohydrates, and other nutrients. And protein always meant eggs, milk and meat in those pictures. Most of us grew up learning science this way. It was never about the quality of protein or quality of carbohydrates or how easily it was digestible or acceptable by our body. In fact, even the quantities or proportions were not explained in details.

Why does nature want us to have a balanced meal? What is meant by a balanced meal? Should each meal be balanced? And how do we measure the balance?

The nature needs balance to exist and we as part of nature too need balance to exist both at physical & mental level. Balance within as well as balance outside.

Balance within the body (results from inputs), balance outside the body (results from our actions and responses) We all know the sufferings when there is an imbalance in any form, including the natural disasters or terrorism.

What we eat becomes us. Then isn't it an obvious thing that what we eat has to be balanced too? And here the balance doesn't mean taking care of only the respective quantities of carbs, proteins and other nutrients, it also means the quality and nature of each food which may or may not provide balance. Quantity, quality, the nature of the food and drink, its impact on us, all should be considered.

And yes, each meal should be balanced. It is not a once in a while requirement. Though our body intelligence always tries, it's best to keep us alive, irrespective of our lifestyle and eating habits, we too should support it.

Each meal plate can be divided into four portions–Carbs 25%, proteins 25%, Vegetables 25% and Raw salads (Vegetables and fruits) 25% for the fibre part. Plant based probiotic drinks or curds added to this meal would add to further benefits.

Please note: This may vary depending on your special health condition hence do ask your doctor or nutritionist

Also, you may refer to last few pages of this book for additional reading and food charts to understand- carbs, proteins, vitamins, minerals and more

How to eat: They say 'Drink your food and chew your water'. Next time your mother says eat fast. Tell her this Ayurvedic ancient principle.

- Food should be made liquid within the mouth. Why? Because digestion happens in the mouth itself when the saliva gets mixed with the food. Depending on the signal that the brain gets on chewing the food, relevant amount of acids are released in the system to break down the food in the stomach. Brain should get a clear signal and correct signal. That's why it is said not to mix raw food and cooked food in the same morsel while eating. Finish raw food first, then have cooked food. Raw is always the priority.
- Similarly, they say chew your water or liquids so that there is enough time for the interaction & information exchange between the brain and the digestive system for efficient digestion. If the food and water is gulped without chewing properly, the digestion can't be efficient as the system gets confused what's coming. Besides when we eat and drink slow, we don't consume more than what is needed by the body because we give time to the body and our inbuilt intelligence system to understand, decide and let us know when we are satiated, when our stomach feels full. But when we eat fast, our system can't understand and

respond so fast and we always end up eating much more than what we need. Things are not so evident when we are young, but our system's processing power wears and tears down with age. It tolerates a lot of things till twenties & thirties but post that we see all signs of aches and pains.

- Most importantly eat in peace and shit in peace. No TV, phone or other distractions while eating or crapping. As the input is important, so is the output. Indigested & stuck food in the body looks worse than the spoilt food left unattended outside for days.
- Bless your food each time you get your plate. Be grateful for the food on your plate. (Example of what you can say when the food comes to you–Thank you God for this meal. Let this meal give me health, happiness and wisdom). You can pray in your language in your words.
- Have food using all your senses. See, touch, taste, smell and listen to your own chewing to observe how much time you have given to each morsel.
- Heaviest meal of the day should ideally be lunch and the smallest meal, the dinner. They say breakfast, but our idea is to give maximum time for healing between two heavy meals, lunch to lunch.
- One of the most important things is to keep a gap of minimum 2-3 hrs between the dinner and sleep time. The sleep is more peaceful and comfortable if one has light dinner and maintains the gap because the gap allows digestion to occur and the contents of the stomach to move into the small intestine, preventing problems like heartburn and insomnia. In the long-term, many larger health issues can be avoided by having a light

meal at night and enough gap before sleeping. The gap needed would largely depend on one's metabolism, age, and digestive health.

When to eat: Only when you feel hungry. That doesn't mean you attend a party at midnight and eat at 1 am due to hunger. Body sends signals as per the body clock that we set. If you stay up late and don't sleep on time obviously, you would get hungry even after dinner because at night the body has to rest, the digestive system has to rest but if the body is not at rest and the brain is active and awake, it is bound to give wrong signals of hunger due to activity. The signal of when to eat would be right when the schedule and the body clock are right, and the body is healthy. If the body is not healthy and there is insulin or leptin resistance in the system, one would get frequent hunger pangs, which are not the sign of actual hunger. So, when the schedule is messed up, or the body is not healthy, you can't expect the body intelligence to function correctly.

How much to eat: Again, listen to the body. When you drink your food, your brain would automatically give you the signal to stop eating once the body's needs are met. Before one feels full, one must stop eating. It's only when the greed takes over the need, problem starts. Also, when it comes to food and nutrition, subtracting and eliminating is better than adding always.

- No one likes shocks. What happens if you are suddenly burdened with a lot of work? Our digestive system too doesn't like shocks. For ex - No breakfast, no lunch but very heavy dinner. Balance would be dividing & eating meals in small portions when hungry. In addition, our digestive system too needs a break from the continuous work load, so giving it a complete rest at regular intervals is a nice thing to do. Fasting once every week or every 15 days not only helps in cleaning but also in healing. Fasting is highly important. This is one reason why most religions have fasting prescribed for the followers.

Points to remember here

- Food determines weight and exercise determines shape. Food has to be corrected first before working on the body.
- Also, please know that the signal of hunger can't be correct if the body clock is not proper, or the body is unhealthy and eating habits are not proper. Frequent hunger can be a sign of more insulin production, leptin resistance or more acidity.

Utensils to use for cooking and storing food

Some metals and materials are better for cooking while others are not and can be toxic. Aluminium can cause harm depending on the quantity that gets mixed with the food on an everyday basis. Teflon (polytetrafluoroethylene) coated non-stick cookware could be toxic when heated at high temperatures as long-term exposure to PFOA (the chemical released by overheating the cookware is linked to a host of conditions from cancer to thyroid disease). Ceramic cookware too can be harmful when ceramic coating is very thin over aluminium metal because ceramic coating can easily erode, leaving aluminium to get exposed.

What to use?

Stainless Steel: Readily available and one of the best for cooking. It retains approximately 60 to 70 percent nutrient content of the food. However, one should refrain from buying the stainless-steel utensil that is polished with chromium or nickel, as those may cause health threats.

Cast Iron: One of the long-lasting and sturdy metals that can be used for non-stick cooking. Small amounts of iron leach from the cookware during cooking, however, that is healthy for us as long as one is not suffering from an overload of iron in the body. Acidic foods should be avoided in case of cast iron.

Glass: Glass is a non-reactive material, which means it neither release harmful elements into the food being cooked nor does it absorb any nutrition from the food, making it one of the safest. The only limitation that is associated with it is that it is mostly used for microwave cooking. For storing purpose, it is great.

Brass: Food prepared in brass utensils retain as much as 90 percent of its nutritional content. However, cleaning these is a task. Also, acidic foods should not be cooked in brass.

Bronze: Bronze is another very healthy medium of cooking food, as this material tends to keep approximately 97 percent of the nutritional quotient of the food intact. However, tin or nickel may be added to the brassware for making utensils, which may lead to health hazards.

Clay Pots: Clay heats up slowly and thus helps in retaining moisture and nutrients of the food intact, making it one of the ideal options. The biggest drawback is the time taken for cooking. And of course, glazed clay pots shouldn't be used as the glaze may have harmful chemicals.

Disclaimer-

You may have a question here. Not everyone can afford a balanced meal. Most farmers and construction workers have primarily carbohydrate rich diets. Yet, they are in a better shape than many. In fact, in many countries people are fitter with less balanced diets. Why? So, the answer lies in their lifestyle, their behaviour and the way their mind and body function. How our body uses the inputs and converts as per the needs depends a lot on our physical and mental nature. For most of us, with a modern sedentary lifestyle balanced diet is definitely one of the solutions unless we start to do works which require a lot of physical aggression. (Ref book–Dove, Diplomats and Diabetes by Milind Watve)

2.1b Water

Water is life. Everything is born out of water. You, me, ... the whole creation. It is more precious than most precious possessions, including gems and jewellery, property and wealth, home and relationships. If we lose everything else, we would still live, but without water, there won't be any life on this planet. Without life, there is no question of anything as precious.

Life happens in water, and even inside mother's womb, that provides and nourishes. Our planet is 70% water and our bodies too, as a reflection, have 70% water. As a matter of fact, our blood contains 83% water, the lean muscle tissue contains 75% water. The most important organ in our body, the brain, contains over 80% of water. Lungs are about 75%, skin is at least 70%, kidneys are about 80% and even the bones have 22% water content.

So, we need to take enough water to maintain our body composition. Let's see how much to drink, when to drink and how to drink.

How much to drink water: Just like food, for water intake as well, listen to your own body. Our thirst is an excellent indicator, provided we maintain a healthy body and routine. Many of us don't even realize when we are thirsty due to our lifestyles. In such cases, it's important to pay attention to our water intake and check the health indicators.

Dryness, inflammation, muscle weakness, constipation, urine colour and no sweat are some of the signs that the body may need more water. If anyone suffers from bigger health issues, do check water intake too for correction.

You would have read or heard many theories about how many glasses to drink, but please understand drinking more or drinking less water both can be harmful. More water puts additional burden on our kidneys and less water puts additional burden on our digestive and excretory system.

Besides, the water requirement of a body would depend on many factors, including climate conditions, amount of activity, type of food, age & so on. So, it's difficult to give a fixed formula. However, the following are broad guidelines on drinking water that can be followed alongside thirst signals.

Drink approx. 1 glass per 10 kg of body weight water per day. Depending on weather and body requirement & comfort, one can drink a little more if required. Always drink in small quantities which feels comfortable to you and slowly not like 5 glasses at once. Go to finish your quota of water per day.

Drinking water first thing in the morning is a therapeutic ritual to clean the system even if one doesn't feel thirsty. Below is the process to be followed.

When to drink water: If you haven't heard of Japanese water therapy or teachings from Ayurveda, here is a simplest solution to clean your system and keep it healthy.

Just like the way we take bath to clean our body from outside, it is absolutely necessary to clean the same body from inside too and what better can there be than the water itself to wash away toxins first thing in the morning.

Process

- After waking up drink 4 x 160ml glasses of water (not cold) before doing anything else, including brushing the teeth.
- After drinking the water, one can brush the teeth, but one shouldn't eat or drink anything for 45 minutes.
- After 45 minutes eat and drink as normal.
- Sick & elderly, or people not used to this, can start this process gradually.

Secondly, after every meal or snack, large quantities of water should be avoided as water dilutes the stomach acid required to digest the food. If possible, avoid drinking water 40 minutes before and 1.5- 2 hrs after the meal. Very small quantities can be taken depending on the food one has taken. Soup and salad may not require you to have water immediately, but yes, cereals come under hard food as there is hardly any water content in cereals, so you may need a few sips.

According to Ayurveda, if one drinks water just before a meal, it causes weakness because water is a natural appetite suppressant; the hunger dies down with water intake so one would eat less than needed by the body. Secondly, the water just before the meal would also neutralize the stomach acid, which is necessary to digest the food coming leading to improper digestion.

If one drinks water just after a meal, that too can lead to obesity because enough time has to be given for stomach acid to function and break down the food. If there is no proper digestion, absorption, and assimilation, obviously the body will bloat.

Small amounts of water during the meal, has a balancing effect or no effect on the health. Remember, small quantities that too, depending on the water content of the food. For foods with water rich content, water may not be needed with the meal but for hard foods it is. Do remember, water should not make one feel boated or heavy in the abdomen.

Apart from meal times, water should be taken regularly. And when there is more activity or exercise, more water is required by the body. An estimated 500 ml of water is needed to compensate for fluid loss for 1 hour of exercise. Muscles regenerate faster and one can overcome muscle strain easier if the body is well hydrated.

How to drink water

- Sip and don't chug - Always drink slowly and in small quantities throughout the day. Sip by sip with a calm mind. Again, like food, even the water needs to be mixed with saliva in our mouth to neutralize the stomach acid. If we don't swish the water in mouth but gulp it, very little saliva would reach the stomach to neutralize the acid and hence the system would remain acidic. So wet your tongue and swish water in the mouth before sipping it down.
- Drink water in sitting position only not while standing up or while lying down. Water is also a food and macronutrient. Ayurveda recommends eating and drinking food while sitting on the ground.
- Ideally avoid too cold water. Lukewarm and room temperature water is the best. When water that is at room temperature or warmer touches the lips, it gives a feeling of satisfaction and signals the body about water intake. If we simply gulp the ice-cold water, it firstly shocks the senses, and in the stomach, it deactivates the needed bacteria for our digestion. Please remember, having cold water with a meal is toxic to the digestion.

What is safe & clean water: United nations have declared access to safe drinking water as the fundamental right of every human being, but how many of us realize that the water we may be using at home through our high-end filters could actually be acidic? From food to water to medicines, misleading advertisements, products and information have caused more harm to us and to our nature than anything.

The best water is the natural water sourced directly from the origin. It provides us with essential salts and minerals and, most importantly it is alkaline in nature. Yes, that's not possible to get that for everyone, so here are a few ways to make water healing, safe, and clean.

Whether you boil the water or use water filters at home, please ensure the following:

- Ph level test - The ideal PH level of water should be between 6 to 8. So don't just check dirt and bacteria in your water but also the Ph level because acidic water on a regular basis can do harm on a long-term basis. Remember, health starts with good digestion and we need an alkaline atmosphere within our bodies for that.
- Secondly, instead of directly using the water from filters, store them in copper or silver vessels. Copper has numerous antioxidants and anti-bacterial properties that help boost the immune system of the body. It also has anti-cancer properties. Water in the silver vessel has the power to remove free radicals from the body and gives a cooling effect in the intestines, and smoothens the process of digestion.
- Also, it is advisable to keep the water vessel under the sun for some time with a net cloth cover so that sun rays can fall directly into the water. This charges the water. Drink sun charged water with the feelings of gratefulness towards the water as a life source.

How to store water

Water should be stored in stainless steel, clay pot, in Brass, bronze, glass, silver or copper pots. Plastic should definitely be avoided. Copper possesses oligodynamic properties which prove fatal to the bacteria and virus present in the water, making it one of the best to prevent health conditions.

2.1c Air

Do you feel different when you go to the jungles or at hill stations or in a park full of trees? We all do, right? We are also nature and the more aligned we are to everything else in the nature, obviously we would feel healthier & happier. Oxygen is another condition of life for us. Just hold your breath for 1 min and you will know. Lack of air will kill us faster than a lack of any other element, so first thing, let's be thankful each time we breathe.

Air infuses our bodies with prana (life energy). We need oxygen in every part of our body including each cell. In the body, air is the force allowing blood to circulate, breath to move, nerve impulses to glide, thoughts to flow, and joints to propel our movement through the world. Air is the force behind all motion. Is it possible to compromise on any of these? No, right?

To start with, low oxygen levels in our system can cause headaches and shortness of breath. The way it happens at high altitudes where the air is thin.

In extreme cases, insufficient oxygen can damage essential organs like the heart and the brain. This is a well-known fact. We have all seen such killings in movies when the air flow is stopped.

The worst is the chronic case of low oxygen levels, which we don't realize on a day today basis. Chronic low oxygen can put stress on the internal organs, increasing the risk of failure. (Stress means the organ is burdened with work to perform without adequate inputs like oxygen) Imagine, you have a slave; you care the least for it, starve it, beat it, burden it with work... what would happen at some point in time? It would collapse. That's what happens to our organs and body.

So, let's learn how to have more oxygen in the system.

First is we need pure air, second is we need to breathe properly so that we inhale as much as possible and third thing is good absorption of oxygen in our system.

How to have more fresh and clean air

- Stay as close to trees and jungles as possible. I realize I am reiterating a well-known fact, yet all of us are running after things not even remotely close and as important as air (the life energy)
- Second option is to visit deep jungles and green hill stations as often as possible
- For people living in cities, at least fill your homes with live plants from inside as well outside.
- To inhale more oxygen and to absorb more oxygen so that each of our organs can function efficiently, one needs better lung capacity. Means no smoking or alcohol. Smoking interferes with our lung function and alcohol interferes with our oxygen absorption. Alcohol can cause breathing disruptions during sleep, reduced oxygen saturation in the blood by affecting the haemoglobin (transporter of oxygen in the body) and agglutination, or clumping, of red blood cells which again impacts the distribution of oxygen within the body.
- Clean & fresh air can heal us, polluted air or less air absorption within our bodies can do the opposite.
- Practice deep breathing techniques and various pranayamas to make the breathing mechanism efficient. Details on how to breathe will follow in the chapter on breathing.

2.1d Thoughts

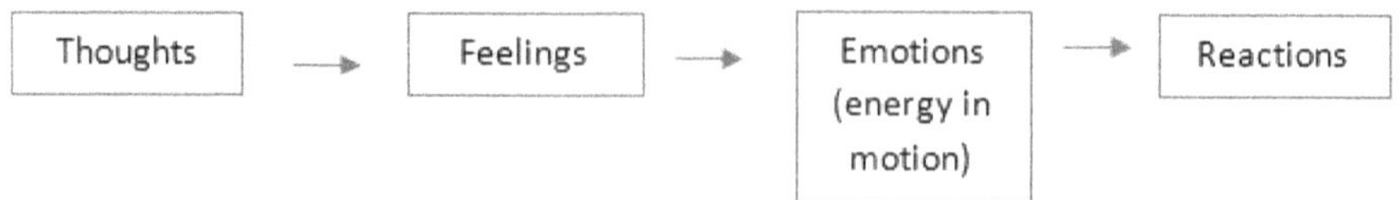

Thoughts lead to feelings; feelings lead to emotions (feelings in motion) and emotions lead to reactions. Our reactions to things (expressed or unexpressed) determine the outcomes. Better outcomes need better action or response, not reactions. Better response needs better emotions. Better emotions result from better feelings and better feelings result from better thoughts. So, it all starts with the thought.

We make our bodies feel good by having better thoughts about ourselves and others. But how to have better thoughts? Thoughts are the result of our mind & consciousness both. While we would learn about mind in details later, let's figure out a few ways to have better thoughts.

Deliberate everyday practice focussed on better thoughts: Engaging in deliberate practice every day focused on cultivating positive thoughts is a transformative endeavour that holds the power to reshape one's mindset and enhance overall well-being. By consciously dedicating time and effort to fostering better thoughts, we embark on a journey of self-discovery and mental fortification. This intentional practice involves consistently redirecting attention towards constructive and optimistic perspectives, challenging negative cognitive patterns, and embracing mindfulness techniques.

We should deliberately think of good things and imagine things that we want in reality irrespective of our day's experience, first thing in the morning and last thing just before sleeping. This is needed during the alpha state of mind (Awake and resting state). Never sleep with any negative thought or emotion because you would get up with the same feeling. Alpha state is the state of creation and manifestation, and we should never think of what we don't want during this state because what we focus on in a relaxed state increases.

This is the time to bless ourselves and our children. Yes, bless yourself. Literally keep your hand on your head and bless yourself with good health, happiness and abundance. Besides, it's a great practice to bless your children at night when you put them to bed or in the morning when you wake them up. Say all positive things about them, let them know that they are a precious gift you are thankful for. Most importantly, use this time to affirm positive qualities in yourself and in others. The words you say at night in the ears of your children go a long way in building their psyche.

Meditation: There are many ways to meditate. Do what suits you, because meditation simply puts you in a state of observation. Meditation provides a sanctuary for individuals to observe their thoughts without judgment and develop a deeper connection with the present moment. When we are an observer and not a participant, the thoughts lose power and dissolve themselves. The act of observation allows us to witness our thoughts without being consumed by them, creating a space for objectivity and introspection. By adopting this mindful stance, we detach ourselves from the emotional entanglements that negative thoughts often carry.

Journaling: Can be used in two ways. One to vent out everything that's inside. This helps one become an observer again. It's like reading your own mind and thought patterns. Journaling provides a safe space to express and process your emotions. Writing down your thoughts can help you make sense of your feelings and gain clarity. And secondly, to affirm and focus on positive thoughts that one can write on a daily basis about yourself, your life and your surroundings. Regularly acknowledging and appreciating the good things can improve overall well-being.

Gratitude: An intentional practice to focus on the good part of your life. It's not about maintaining saintly; it's actually caring for our own well-being. There are 100 things which don't happen the way we want them to in our heads and, of course, our brains are occupied with all those imperfections throughout the day, whether we are conscious of it or not. Hence, it's absolutely essential to focus on whatever you are thankful for (whatever means good to you in your head). This way at least some part of the day, we would generate good feelings.

The company we keep: Change your company to have better thoughts. Your company is not just your friends circle, your office colleagues but also the books you read, the movies or TV series you watch, the people you listen to through videos or forums, people you follow on YouTube or twitter or in your society, people you learn things from including the classes you attend. Your company is everything that can or may have an influence on you. So please make sure you choose your company wisely, because everything that we see or listen to or speak influences. It influences us and others in many ways, some we realize, some we don't even realize.

Surrounding ourselves with individuals who inspire and challenge us can foster personal development. Positive role models can encourage us to set and achieve goals, learn new skills, and strive for excellence.

Am sure you would agree, not just innocent children, but we make so many of our choices based on the ads despite knowing that they may be exaggerated selling efforts. It is because our subconscious mind picks up a lot more than we can imagine as true without filtering from the exposure it gets. So, here we have an option… option to choose our company while there are all kinds of influences in this world. Which choice to make? The choice that supports our progress, our long-term joy & peace.

Our Food and lifestyle: Yes, our food and lifestyle influence our thoughts big time. Everything is interlinked and interconnected in this universe. That's why it is said every action has an equal and opposite reaction. Covid time has been an excellent teacher to prove that. Every action we take, every thought we think, everything that we do or don't has an impact and a reaction in this universe. It's just that we don't get to see the complete effect from our relative position as a participant in this world. All of us have read food gives us energy, but very few people have gone beyond that point. Important question is what kind of energy? Most of us take food as something that our tongue should like and that fills our stomach, but that's not all. In fact, the energy that we receive from what we eat and drink is the most important thing. And our food choices should be based on the kind of energy we need.

To respond to life from a balanced state of mind, we need the energy that keeps us in a balanced state, the energy which makes us do good to ourselves and others, the energy that can help fulfil our purpose of birth.

However, different foods and drinks have different energies. Anything that's put us in a state of imbalance or extreme, for example, too sweet, too sour, too hot, too cold, too spicy, may not be good. Alcohol and drugs again take us towards huge highs and lows (imbalance again).

Vegan, vegetarian and non-vegetarian food also carry different energy and hence impact our body and mind differently.

As mentioned before, emotions are energies in motion. The level of emotional complexity increases from plants to animals to human beings. Human beings have mind of their own, unlike plants and animals. If we kill another human to eat, we absorb the highest amount of emotion that being would be carrying. If we kill an animal, we would absorb its emotional energy (extreme fear and pain at the time of being killed). So not just physically (due to large intestines that humans have, which is not meant for meat) but also at an energetic level, we create imbalance when we eat animal meat.

Our need for food shouldn't be the cause of someone's pain. Plants meet our needs when we eat plant-based food to survive, but eating animals with higher emotional energy is only due to our greed. Yes, when we were not evolved, we were more like animals; we ate animals, but now we are evolved and civilized, moving from survival state to more evolved states of love and compassion.

Eating another life full of emotions in the name of a high protein diet for good body… does it make sense? Shouldn't we be beautiful and balanced from inside first, especially when there are plant-based options available?

Second comes the lifestyle–Balance in lifestyle creates balance in our body and in mind. Achieving balance in lifestyle is fundamental to fostering equilibrium in both our physical well-being and mental health. Respecting body clock, peaceful sleep, exercising, exposure to morning sun on an everyday basis and keeping our work life balance. Nothing more, nothing less. A harmonious lifestyle encompasses various elements such as a nutritious diet, regular exercise, sufficient rest, and mindful activities. When we strike a balance between work and leisure, prioritize self-care, and nurture positive relationships, we create a foundation for overall well-being.

The keyword is balance. And the best way to understand the balance is to check if something is a need or a greed or a compulsion. If any habit or behaviour arises out of a greed or a compulsion, imbalance is bound to happen, including the corporate rat race or social media nonsense. A balanced lifestyle promotes mental clarity, emotional stability, and resilience in the face of life's challenges. It allows us to navigate stress more effectively, leading to a sense of calm and tranquillity.

External environment & Surroundings: Our environment and surroundings play quite an important role in determining our quality of thoughts. The spaces we inhabit, the people we interact with, and the overall ambiance of our surroundings contribute to the mental atmosphere we experience. By curating our surroundings to reflect positivity and tranquillity, we create a conducive space for constructive thoughts and emotional balance. Additionally, connecting with nature, embracing natural settings, and incorporating conscious way of living into our environment can further enhance the quality of our thoughts, promoting mental clarity and a more positive outlook on life.

A. **Decluttering**: For clarity of thoughts, it's good to declutter from time and again and throw away all unnecessary stuff which is no longer in use. Decluttering holds significant importance in fostering a sense of order, efficiency, and overall well-being in both our physical and mental spaces. This not only enhances visual aesthetics but also promotes a smoother flow of daily activities, reducing the stress associated with a cluttered space. The act of decluttering itself can be therapeutic, helping individuals let go of unnecessary possessions and distractions, and creating space for a more intentional and purposeful life. It allows for better decision-making, improved productivity, and a reduced sense of overwhelm.

B. **Natural living for ideas and inspiration**: Humans have been made to stay as close to green covers as possible, not just for fresh air and water sake but also for good thoughts, inspiration and ideas. Don't we feel better in the garden, jungles and forests? Natural living for creativity, ideas and inspiration holds immense importance . Natural living also encourages a more sustainable and mindful lifestyle, aligning with a broader sense of connectedness to the environment.

While this may not be practically possible for all in the present times, one can try to live naturally, use natural products as much as possible. And avoid using products very often that produce electromagnetic waves and can interfere with our wellbeing. Our thoughts depend on our wellbeing. Embracing a natural way of living not only nurtures our physical well-being but also serves as a powerful catalyst for generating ideas and finding inspiration. Hence following can help.

- Staying away from telecom towers.
- Switching off the Wi-Fi at least before sleeping.
- Reducing the usage of microwaves etc.
- Switching off mobile phones and TV at least 1 hour before sleeping. The earlier, the better. Similarly, checking your mobile first thing in the morning is not a good way to start the day. First, you should plan your day in your head and then let the day unfold.
- Not sleeping next to the mobile and keeping the mobile phone in a case to avoid direct contact with the body as far as possible.
- Consciously trying to reduce the use of chemicals to protect ourselves and our environment.
- Make your home green. Bring in as many plants as possible.

2.2 OUR MINDS

Body impacts mind, and the mind impacts the body. The two are inseparable. What is the mind? Is it any organ inside us? It is something outside of us? Is it the inbuilt intelligence?

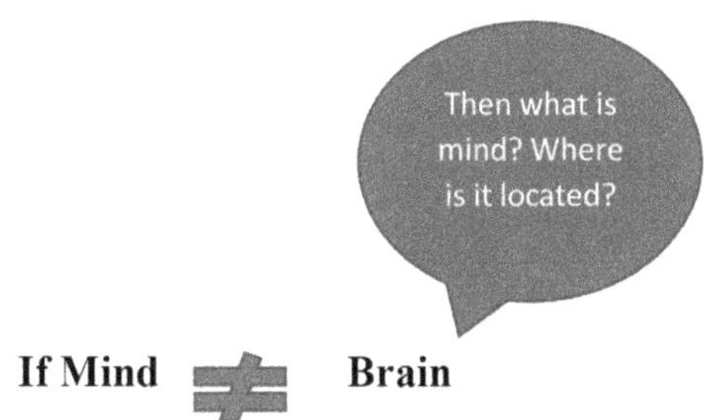

Mind is a formless and non-physical faculty that influences the way we understand, perceive, think about and act or react to everything. It includes the interpretations and meanings that we give to events as well as the identification with our personality. Many philosophies and religions have given the name Karma to it.

Mind is not inbuilt intelligence. The mind works through the brain. It is energy, and it creates energy through thinking, feeling, and choosing. The mind uses the brain, and the brain responds to the mind. Mind (our thinking pattern) can even change the brain structure, as we call it neuroplasticity.

Mind is what separates one from the other. If the mind is not there, each one of us will have just pure intelligence aligned to the laws of nature. For example, if all of us are simple computers, we would have the same program to function in a standard way.

Let's understand the mind

You as a child got chocolate whenever mom was happy with your behaviour. You interpreted getting chocolate as a reward. You may also interpret that getting chocolate means you are good enough. You may also interpret having sweets means happiness given that your taste buds liked it. You associate chocolate with happiness. This is part one.

The day someone denies you a chocolate, you give meaning to that event after referring to your past experience. No chocolate means no reward, not good enough, no happiness, conclusion I am sad. This is part two.

You choose to feel bad and cry as a reaction to not getting a chocolate. This is part three.

All this happens in our mind & because of our mind. So, the quality of our thoughts depends on how our mind perceives & concludes. So, there is a vicious circle of thinking, feeling, and choosing.

Now how do we ensure that our mind supports us to think good, feel good & choose good? After all, we all want to be in a state of joy & bliss.

a. Either only good things should happen to us, your good as you understand and my good as I understand. We should always get the chocolate. This is obviously not possible, as we go through many different experiences both good and bad, in our eyes.
b. Or second option is that we change the way we see or look at things. The way we give the meaning of good and bad to what happens. Not getting a chocolate could also mean something better is coming. It may mean more happiness as sugar is not very good in the long term. This is just an example. Through our understanding, wisdom & awareness, we can change our interpretations of what we experience in life so as to make better choices and take needed actions instead of reactions. This is influencing at the level of thinking & feeling.

Another example–Let's talk about the meaning of beauty. Who has said being fairer is beautiful? It is only the meaning that we have given. Every country has a different meaning of beauty. For Burmese, it is a long neck, for Africans it is thick lips, for Indians it could be eyes like Aishwarya. It is all about meanings that we give to the things, and meanings can be changed to support us. We can choose meanings that serve us well. Being an Indian, if I have thick lips, why can't I choose the African beauty standard to think about myself? They say thick lips are beautiful, so I am beautiful. Here, the most important factor would be you and not what others think, the society thinks. You can change your meanings for your life, not the meanings that others hold. Also, one can't manipulate like killing others is good or having junk food is good because we are all bound by the laws of nature. Going against nature means going against ourselves.

c. Or the third option, we start taking everything in the same spirit. Whatever happens, you don't react to good and bad feelings or sensations in the body. You learn to accept everything as it is, irrespective of the meanings that you have given to things. Whether you get chocolate or not, you train your brain not to react to different sensations or feelings. You can be still irrespective of what life gives. Not very easy, but possible by training. This is the influence, at the level of choosing. Reality is always neutral. We give the meaning of good and bad to it. If we take something as good, then bad also exists for us as the absence of good. When we take things as it is, we are in the present.

One can train/teach the brain to take everything in the same way. That's what Buddha taught in his Vipassana teachings. This doesn't mean suppression of feelings at all or distracting your mind towards other things. It simply means observing everything as it is without reacting.

In Vipassana, we start with observing each sensation in our body, pay attention to each point in our body, become aware and then and treat all points of sensations as same. This increased awareness allows individuals to observe their mental and physical processes objectively, leading to a deeper understanding of their inner workings. Basically, teach the brain not to react to the good and bad sensations in the body while meditating in sitting position for long when the body comes up with pain, too. This leads to pure awareness and expansion of consciousness when we stop following the mind, irrespective of what it says, and train it to keep still while observing all.

What happens when we observe things as they are? Let me explain with an example. Say, you are in a wedding; you take various pictures and see someone is eating, someone is on stage, someone is talking in a group, someone is dancing etc, etc. You see things in bits and pieces because the scene in front of you depends on your relative position.

However, if you want to see the whole wedding at a specific moment, every person and everything in it, you need to use a drone camera which can take the complete picture of the scene. One can't be part of the scene to understand the complete scene, right? So how do we understand the whole world and beyond, starting with ourselves? We need to become observers and be distant from the scene. When we can see the complete picture as an observer outside of it by not participating in it, we would be in a better position to act. That's why most meditations teach us to become an observer first so that our ability to see a complete scene improves. And we always start small, so instead of the world, we start the practice with our body.

There are various other meditation process which can help reach this stage just that the point of attention may differ. It can be breath, it can be heart, it can be a mantra or name or anything or even a physical idol just to make it easier to put the attention to.

Not just meditation, there are many other ways of self-exploration and one is free to choose based on trials and errors whatever feels right & suitable.

The path we choose is up to us–prayer, surrender, devotion, mantra, tantra, Kriya whatever. Idea is to become less instinctive and more conscious of what we choose to do. End result should be actions and not reactions for better outcomes. We are all working towards being good at life, right?

Summary - How to work with the mind

Working with the mind is an ongoing process that involves working towards self-awareness, intentional practices, and a commitment to personal growth. Mind can be influenced at two levels primarily, as explained above, so that we act with wisdom and not react due to emotions. As they say, life is 10% what happens to us and 90% how we react to what happens. Our reactions are our choices. How can these choices be correct in the context?

a. Influencing the thinking & feeling part in mind–Here, we change the way we perceive things for our good and others good as explained above (Give meanings that support our feeling ok towards the events of life–a deliberate practice) so that responses and choices are balanced. At least become conscious of what's going on in our minds and become careful in giving the meanings. This also helps in developing resilience.

b. Influencing the choosing part in mind - We look at everything as it is without getting affected or attached. No reaction. This needs training the brain to avoid auto reflexes & reactions as the brain manifests the mind's energy. Taking pauses and then responding when our brain and body are calm and composed.

Moral of the story is our choice/free will should come from a point of good intention, awareness and balance, not as per what the monkey mind forces one to do at the heat of a moment.

There are many ways to influence the thinking, feeling and choosing as per our scriptures, from meditation to striving for self-knowledge, to practicing detachment in every action, to devotion towards the creator to working with body and breath, so on and so forth. Everything requires daily practice and intent.

There is so much scope of improvement in us that when we sort one thing a day, 100 things crop up the next day, making us feel that we haven't progressed at all. But can personally assert that change does happen. It's like cleaning. When the first layer is removed, we get to see many more. The idea is not to stop cleaning. 1/1000th of an improvement a day is also good enough as long as we are moving forward every day.

In the next chapter, let's dig deeper on how breath can help influence our mind.

2.3 BREATH

↑

Breath is the connection between

The connection between mind and body: **Body is physical, mind is nonphysical. Breath is the life energy that connects the body to the mind** (the personality, the associations, the perceptions, the impressions that we carry, etc.)

As long as we breathe, we are alive, so breath is connected to the body. It is the life source. Similarly, all of us have observed that our breathing pattern changes with our emotions. Heart beats faster due to faster breathing, especially when we are upset or anxious or angry, so breath is connected to the mind too because emotional response depends on the mind (perceptions).

It is also observed that when we our breathing is slow, calm and rhythmic, we automatically come to a better relaxed emotional state. We can use our breath to work both with our body and mind, to bring balance physically and mentally, to have balanced responses.

Scientifically, let's understand our emotional & physical relaxed and non-relaxed states and how can breathing help.

We have two kinds of nervous systems (sympathetic and parasympathetic) to control our involuntary and reflexive functions of the human body and, in turn our responses. The sympathetic and parasympathetic systems work in a coordinated manner to maintain physiological balance. They often have opposing effects on the same organs or systems, allowing for precise control and fine-tuning of bodily functions based on the body's needs at any given moment. The balance between these two systems is crucial for overall health and homeostasis.

The sympathetic nervous system is the driving force behind the **'fight or flight'** response and triggers a number of physiological changes that prepare the body to confront or flee a perceived threat. So when SNS is activated in us, we would be anxious, not relaxed, there would be a release of adrenaline, higher heart rate & blood pressure and more glucose would be generated because sudden rush of energy is needed for both fight or flight which are extreme responses.

We don't need this physical state or such extreme responses all the time. This state is once in a while need only when there is serious danger but unfortunately in present times we are mostly in this fight-or-flight mode.

The para sympathetic nervous system, on the other hand controls the **'rest and digest' or 'feed and breed'** functions of the body and maintains the body's internal environment while keeping heart rate and blood pressure steady. We need this state more often when our muscles are relaxed, heart rate is low, digestion and metabolism are efficient. This state is a more balanced and calm state. This is when our emotional response can be calm, not an extreme response like fight or flight.

Based on various researches and experiments, it has been found that the parasympathetic nervous system is activated by slow, deep & rhythmic breathing. Scientists have found that the vagus nerve, a nerve that connects the heart, lungs and digestive tract with the brain by way of the parasympathetic nervous system, sends signals to the brain to relax and restore when the parasympathetic nervous system is activated.

Which means controlled & regulated breathing can change our response from fight and flight to rest & digestion (a balanced state of body& brain). Balanced physical state, in turn, brings balance to mind. As the mind affects body, the body too affects the mind.

How to use breath to bring balance in the body and mind

Using breath to bring balance to the body and mind is a fundamental aspect of any mindfulness and relaxation techniques.

- Regular breathing exercises - including Deep Breathing; Abdominal Breathing; Equal Breathing; Mindful Breathing; Alternate Nostril Breathing; 4-7-8 Breathing; Box Breathing; yoga and pranayama can be practiced to regulate breathing and activate the parasympathetic nervous system.
- Consciously correcting the breathing pattern throughout the day is an excellent practice for promoting relaxation, reducing stress, and enhancing overall well-being.
- Last but not least, practice deep breathing when feeling anxious or angry or scared. Any emotional extreme can be handled with slow and deep breathing. True, the difficult part is to remember in the heat of the moment, but this is one way to change the response and reaction by practice.

Deep breathing activates the parasympathetic nervous system, promoting a relaxation response. It provides a pause between the stimulus and your reaction, allowing you to respond more thoughtfully to a situation. Deep breathing helps relax the physical responses, promoting a sense of calm and preventing the escalation of anger. It empowers you to take control of your physiological and emotional responses, providing a valuable skill for managing challenging moments in a healthier way.

Learning – Listen to your body (organ system), listen to your heart (organ), listen to your gut (organ). Don't listen to the mind all the time, it can be misleading.

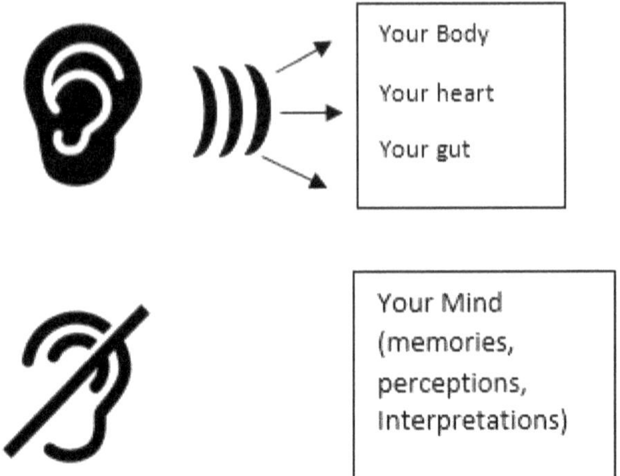

Mind is not an organ. Mind is our perceptions, our associations and our interpretations or meanings we have given to events. If everything is changing all the time, including billions of new cells which are formed every day in our bodies, how relevant is it to see 'now' with an old lens? We need fresh lens every time not just to see ourselves but others too.

Mind can project anything, but what we do with that information depends purely on our wisdom. The human mind is incredibly complex and capable of imagination, creativity, and the generation of various ideas and possibilities. The role of wisdom becomes crucial in guiding our actions and decisions based on the information and projections our minds generate. Wisdom involves a deep understanding of the implications and consequences of our choices, as well as the ability to make sound judgments.

Having the ability to project ideas or possibilities is one aspect of the mind's capabilities, but the responsible and thoughtful use of that information is where wisdom comes into play. Developing wisdom involves cultivating critical thinking, emotional intelligence, empathy, and a broader understanding of the world and its complexities. It's the application of this wisdom that shapes our behaviours and decisions, influencing the outcomes of our actions.

2.4 BETTER DECISION MAKING OR CHOOSING–HOW?

By using body, breath and mind, we work on ourselves and prepare ourselves for better insight and intuition, to choose better responses to life events.

Insight + Intuition ⟶ Wisdom

So, we should to be guided by our wisdom when choosing anything or deciding anything and not by the whims and fancies of mind. Wisdom incorporates various aspects, including knowledge, experience, critical thinking, and a sense of morality. When we rely on wisdom, we are more likely to make informed and thoughtful decisions that take into account the potential consequences and ethical considerations.

Wisdom = Making right choices/taking right actions in the present context based on a good judgment of future consequences.

It is the sum total of insight that is awareness or consciousness and intuition that is the gut feel or the voice within.

Insight involves a deep and penetrating understanding of situations, people, or issues. It often comes from a combination of knowledge, awareness, experience, and reflective thinking. Insight allows individuals to see beyond the surface and grasp the underlying truths.

Often described as the 'gut feeling' or an inner voice, intuition involves a quick and instinctive understanding or judgment. It's a form of knowledge that may not be consciously reasoned but is felt or sensed. Intuition can be influenced by one's experiences and the subconscious processing of information.

Most importantly, developing intuition and insight needs focus & clarity in mind, i.e., not mixing emotions. An emotionally driven person can't make a good judgement in most cases.

Let me clarify here. We have all understood an emotional person as someone who is empathetic and sensitive. That's not true. Anger is a major emotion and how do people react when filled with emotion called anger? Like fools, right?

Most blunders or crimes from rape to murder to world wars happen because of emotional outbreaks. Being very emotional or emotionally driven is not a compliment. Being intuitive is, being empathetic is, being insightful is. So, to improve intuition or insight, to be a good decision maker, we all need to handle our emotions well and learn not to operate out of emotions but to be in a state of balance to decide and act. And we have already learnt that a healthy mind and body leads to balance and clarity.

Wisdom-Intuition/Insight → comes from → Clarity in thinking (Balance) → comes from → Healthy mind & body

There was a time when I used to value educational degrees, power, position etc. and didn't understand the importance of insight or intuition because that's how most of us are brought up. That's what we see all around. We see the social race.

It took quite long for me to understand that wisdom is intelligence within us which doesn't require education and education/ power or position doesn't guarantee wisdom.

Education can help, but wisdom is something we all can develop without any formal degree.

I can think of an example from my own life here. This happened when I was in class fourth. It's weird, but then I remain very thankful to myself (the wisdom within) for that day.

So, this was around the last period in the school one day, just before the school would end. We were free and didn't have any music class. My music teacher suddenly called me to the music room for no reason. I went in and then I saw him closing the door behind.

Not sure what came upon me, I immediately told him that I urgently needed to go and use the wash-room. He had to open the door, and I never went back.

As I said I was in class fourth and had no education on sexual abuse. In those days, neither the parents nor the school spoke about such things in the childhood phase. It was just my sense or gut feeling which helped to decide what to say & when before I could even get a clue or sign of any misbehaviour. Later I heard stories about him from other kids, though none of us understood anything at that time given that we were too young and studying in a very small hill station in MP.

Intuition or gut feel is like God staying within us and guiding us if only we stay in touch with ourselves and start listening to the voice within. We should acknowledge the value of staying in touch with oneself, being mindful, and listening to the inner voice. Whether viewed as a connection to a higher power or as a product of our internal wisdom, intuition can play a role in decision-making and navigating life's challenges. It's a deeply personal aspect of human experience, and individuals often find their own ways to interpret and integrate intuition into their lives.

Whether it is in the corporate world, in personal life or sports, most of the decisions require insight & intuition both because we all need to decide based on our predictions of future consequences. The combination of insight and intuition is a dynamic process that can enhance decision-making. While insight provides a rational and analytical approach, intuition can offer a more holistic and immediate understanding. Striking a balance between these two aspects can lead to well-rounded decisions, especially in complex and ambiguous situations where predictions about the future are challenging.

Remember 2011 world cup when Dhoni decided to bat amid trouble and India's position didn't look strong. Virender Sehwag went for a duck and Sachin Tendulkar contributing only 18. Dhoni came in and carted the Sri Lankan bowlers around to score 91 not out of 79 balls and in Yuvraj Singh's company, carried India to a six-wicket victory. That decision was a bold decision. What made him decide to take the charge at that time?

Things could have been the other way too and if it were, Dhoni would have received all the blame and anger from the same Indian public which holds him high till date. That was his trust in the voice within.

Now let's look at the business world. In many investigations, it has become clear that intuition plays a great part in today's world of business. In fact, that's the biggest difference between a manager and a leader: a manager relies entirely on concrete facts, such as Excel data, past experience, bookish references etc, whereas a leader is someone who is also willing to decide intuitively in certain situations - even if that entails a risk. **Great leader needs great insight as well as intuition.** Balancing insight and intuition is key for leaders.

The ability to blend analytical thinking with a sense of intuition allows leaders to navigate complex and dynamic environments. It's about making informed decisions based on a solid understanding of the situation while also being responsive to the human and unpredictable aspects of leadership.

Do you know some of the greatest business decision in the history could actually be termed crazy because the facts or figures did not back them? They were based on just intuition /gut feel.

In 1914, when Henry Ford faced falling demand for his cars and high worker turnover, he doubled his employees' wages. Crazy, right? Anyone would think of reducing the cost first. However, within a year, turnover dropped by a factor of more than 20 because of which productivity nearly doubled, and demand for Ford cars boomed because Ford's own workers could now afford the product they were making. This may not work in every company, but Mr Ford's intuition was right.

Another case is about Bill Allen, the CEO of Boeing in the 1950s, who decided to build his own commercial jet when the company was strictly into making planes for the defence industry. He was sure that civilian air travel soon would be a booming industry, which made him bet on the future of Boeing and convince his board to risk $16 million on a new transcontinental airliner, the 707. The move based on his intuition transformed Boeing and air travel forever.

Let's understand the role of insight and intuition better with an example.

Let's say you are a class 5th teacher and you need to decide on a social project based on the number of girls who are regular in school with 95% attendance and will be attending school next year assuming you can't get exact data now. What do you need for this?

Insight or Awareness about number of girls regular in the school, meaning you would need to check in every class or ask each class teacher or check the registers. Your awareness has to move from just class 5th to the whole school as you need a complete picture.

Secondly, you need Intuition about who may attend next year too and who may drop out. You may get some data but you would need to take a chance basis your feeling. The more expanded awareness you have about each class and the more refined your intuition is, the better equipped you will be to decide on the project.

Insight–Expanding awareness

Intuition–Paying attention to the voice within

2.4a Increasing awareness & developing intuition – How?

Sit quietly where no one and nothing can disturb. Close your eyes, take a few deep breaths. Now try focusing on a small part of your body, say nose, where you will get sensations there with every breath. At that point, you become conscious of that part, aware of that part.

Now move your attention from that part to other parts of the body one by one. You would start to feel sensations throughout which means you become aware of the whole body, conscious of the whole body.

Yes, you know you have a body, but unless there is a pain or discomfort, most of us never feel such sensations or don't realize the presence of each and every part of the body. We need to pay focused attention to every point in our body to be conscious of it or aware of it.

Similarly, in our world and beyond, we need to pay focused attention to be conscious of everything there is. We need our awareness or consciousness to move from the specific point in our body to the complete body to our surroundings, to people around, to the whole world, everything in it, and beyond. This is what they say is consciousness expansion or increasing awareness.

Consciousness expansion is heightened or altered state of awareness, perception, or understanding that goes beyond ordinary everyday experiences.

Intuition too demands attention to the voice within. And don't forget that everything starts with using mind, body and breath.

Desires – We all want to be more, have more and do more. The creation is in the state of constant expansion. We are thinking and we are creating. As long as we are alive, there will always be the desire (good or bad). The desire for spiritual progress also is a desire to be more. How to be more and have more especially when it should not only do good to self but to everyone else? Small, consistent actions can lead to significant positive changes over time. The aim should be to strive for a life that not only brings personal fulfilment but also contributes positively to the well-being of the broader community and the world.

One way to be more and have more would be to expand our thinking. Expanding our thinking is a powerful way to open up new possibilities, foster personal growth, and achieve more in various aspects of life. It is an ongoing process that involves self- reflection, continuous learning, and a commitment to personal development. By embracing a mindset of growth and possibility, we can unlock new doors and create a more fulfilling and successful life.

Say for example if you have to feed yourself you would simply pluck the fruit from the tree but if you need to feed your family, you would think of growing the fruit tree and if you have to feed the community, you would think of creating a garden full of fruit trees.

People who create big impacts, don't limit their thoughts to themselves. The expansion of mind needs the thoughts centred around self to move from the self to others and beyond. The expansion of the mind often involves a shift from self-centred thoughts to a broader focus that encompasses others and extends beyond the self. This transition from self-awareness to awareness of others and the broader world is associated with personal growth, empathy, and a deeper understanding of interconnectedness. Not forgetting the self, growth does need thinking bigger and for larger meaning including others good too in our thoughts and plans.

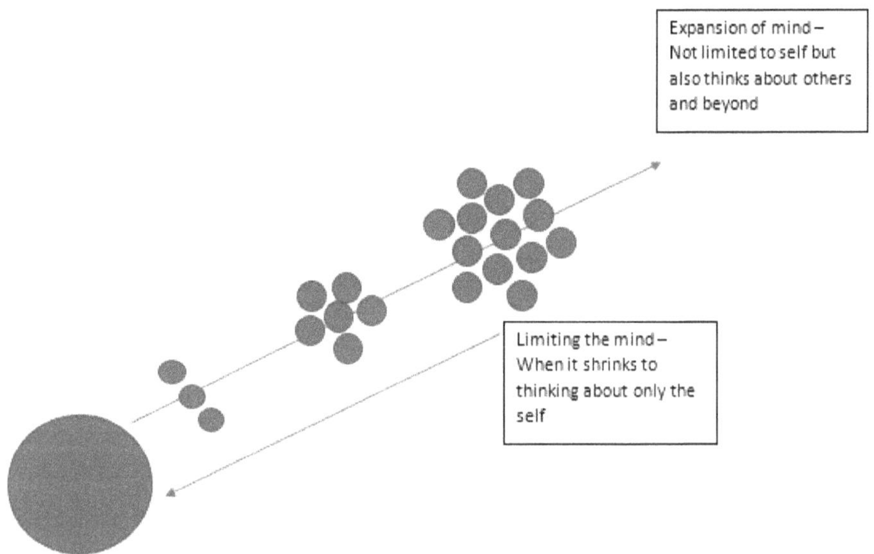

Even for a business to succeed, it has to solve the problem of others. The bigger the problem we solve and for as many people as possible, we grow automatically in our business.

Part 3

Our Duties

If I had an option, I would not allow anyone to be called by his religion. No Hindu, no Muslim, no Christian. Nature created us and we are all governed by the laws of nature (this existence or universe). So, I believe, we only need to practice becoming a human being and follow the religion of humanity by fulfilling the duties of dharma that can help create and maintain the balance within and outside.

As they say, great power comes with great responsibility, hence we humans with more evolved brains obviously have higher responsibility or dharma to be fulfilled in this existence. However, despite the fact, that we hardly have any clarity or intention towards our dharma. We usually talk more about the rights and less about the duty. In fact, blaming the creator so-called Mr God, or conveniently shifting from what our heart says to what our mind says is much easier than accepting & fulfilling our duty.

It's a misnomer. It's a mistake in the first place to assume that we all understand what our dharma is. While no one else is in a position to define dharma for the other, here are general guidelines for every human being given in some of the scriptures so let's learn the basics of religion called humanity.

3.1 DHARMA TOWARDS SELF

Our first dharma or duty is towards ourselves as human beings. A human being is a body, mind and the life energy (that keeps us alive). We need to take care of all–the body, the mind and the life energy because our physical, mental and spiritual well-being is our responsibility. Health is our responsibility, mental clarity is our responsibility, and our choices and reactions is our responsibility. All of us have life purpose to fulfil and so we need our body, mind and energy to support us all along.

Body-To be healthy, all the body inputs food, water, air and thoughts have to be right as discussed in the previous chapter, and we need to work on all levels. We are a combination of everything. Even to treat a physical problem, a human being should be looked at as a whole, all the inputs should be checked to arrive at any conclusion. How to eat and drink, when to eat & drink, how much to eat & how much to drink, everything matters. Our breathing pattern, our thinking pattern, everything is equally important to be taken care of.

Mind–Everything happens in the mind first. The clichéd remark, but true. Mind is behind all pains and gains and how can we as humans afford to become its slave? We need to know the ways to keep ourselves physically healthy, and our minds, too. Yes, it's not an easy thing. It is a basic necessity and every small effort towards mind work goes a long way. It's a long journey, but it starts with the small step of acknowledging that the mind is a monkey and it can't be your master, so you keep the right of choosing consciously to yourself instead of showing compulsive behaviours led by the mind. Who likes to be under a monkey as the boss?

Life energy–This is what gives us the fuel to live and go on. The level of energy in us varies due to many factors physical as well as mental. We have finite energy and so we need to use our energies judiciously. No life energy means dead of course. Lacking life energy means physical diseases, mental irritation or even depression and less productivity.

Energy is not just the start of life but is the reason behind each and every idea, thought, action and creation. The more life energy we have, the better we feel and respond to life events, hence we need to conserve our energies. No point wasting it on useless things or people that don't really matter in our lives.

Invest your energy just the way you invest money in order to get good returns. Example: Someone on the road misbehaved with you. You kept thinking for 30 minutes or more about that person, feeling bad. Thought is an energy, so 30 minutes of the energy is wasted on someone who wasn't important in your life. If those 30 minutes you had spent on talking to your kid who was there with you in the car, you would have gained back some more energy.

Things and people also give energy provided the investment is right. We can't avoid people and situation but how much energy to spend on them is our choice irrespectively.

Mother-in-law hurt you, boss shouted, teenager misbehaved - No point wasting hours of energy thinking about them and feeling negative. Loss of energy is a bigger loss than loss of wealth and money.

Apart from this, there are ways to improve life energy, too. Whatever experience makes you feel good, from deep breathing to going into jungles, to playing with your dog, to writing, to singing a song, to traveling. Do that! Do that to increase your life energy. Choose a lifestyle that conserves your energy or helps you gain more energy because everything has a cost in terms of energy.

For example, If I want to be a country's prime minister, I should be prepared to give the cost in terms of huge energy loss because of so many painful events people plus the mess-ups that are part of the game unless I keep increasing my energy levels in other ways.

So, be aware of the cost that one needs to pay for a specific choice, including parenthood or else diligently work on your practice to generate higher energy levels.

Physical exercising, deep breathing, focus and meditation are some ways to improve energy levels as these help you put the attention to yourself and to your energy within. Obviously, what you focus on increases.

Once again, all this is to choose better and act better because our choice and our actions is our biggest responsibility. Making thoughtful and ethical choices, coupled with responsible actions, is indeed a significant aspect of individual responsibility. The idea of choosing better and acting better reflects a commitment to personal excellence and ethical conduct.

By recognizing the impact of our choices and taking responsibility for our actions, we contribute to our own well-being and the well-being of the broader community. We can only choose and act better when we have a healthy body, healthy mind and lots of life energy to do the right thing that deems fit in a situation.

3.2 DHARMA TOWARDS–THE CREATOR, PARENTS, TEACHERS, CHILDREN, FELLOW HUMAN BEINGS AND SOCIETY AT LARGE.

3.2a Dharma towards the creator

Am not going to talk about any religion but I believe God means goodness within us. When we pray to God, we focus on the goodness within us so that it increases. When we pray to the creator, we pray to the creator within us. Don't we create? We do all the time.

Our lives are our creation. God exists because we want goodness to exist. We want pure love, the highest intelligence, and wisdom to exist. We want this creation to exist. And hence we do have a duty towards God or the creator within all of us.

And think of it what should be our dharma towards the creator?

It would be moving from hatred to pure love, moving from darkness of minds towards the knowledge and wisdom and that's why we need to focus on these qualities on an everyday basis. The way to give attention and focus on goodness and the creator within is completely our choice, but the qualities to focus on are what we should always remember: pure love and the highest wisdom. No religion should take us in the opposite direction.

3.2b Dharma towards our children

Parents' responsibility towards their children always comes first before we can even talk about the dharma of children towards their parents. Parents have the duty to work towards the welfare of their progeny from the time of their conception. Parents must perform all the sacraments for the children, introducing them to worldly living and, educating them either personally or with the help of learned teachers. Through their actions & habits, parents need to fulfil their duties and responsibilities towards their children.

Chanakya, the ancient Indian teacher suggested that parents should tailor their approach to parenting based on the developmental stage and needs of their children. For instance, during the early years till the age of 7 years, he emphasized the importance of affection and nurturing to foster a strong bond between parents and young children. As the child grows older, Chanakya advocated for gradually introducing discipline, value system and education, guiding them towards moral and ethical values. However, once the child reaches 15-16 years of age, he suggests instilling independence and responsibility in children as they mature, preparing them to navigate the challenges of adulthood with wisdom and integrity.

Every stage comes with its own challenges especially the teenage years when the child needs to learn the value of discipline.

Children learn through observation (of parents' actions and reactions) and through absorption (parents' energy expressed or unexpressed). So, parents need to create the right environment, and firm boundaries within themselves to help children grow and become virtuous individuals. Most importantly, give children unconditional love (it's not pampering) without expecting returns.

Parenting has been one of the hardest lessons in my life and I guess I would keep faulting and learning till the end of my life. I agree all the above doesn't come easy as we are talking about teaching through own actions, habits and personal boundaries yet there is no choice but to learn with the intention to do this part right because it is the biggest job role of being human.

Bringing up a child is a continuous learning process for parents. It's not about fixing children; it's about fixing the self and achieving the balance within first. Children also come as parents' teachers, and the challenges posed by them always bring parents' weaknesses to the surface. Unless parents learn the lesson and gain wisdom to overcome their own weaknesses, the dharma is difficult to fulfil in the journey called bringing up children.

In present times, a lot of patience and continuous effort towards taking a balanced approach is required of a parent. No extremes because as mentioned before, everything & everyone keeps changing, so what's the point in concluding or labelling?

A dacoit can change into a sage, a school dropout can own & run a company where most educated people may work under him. A student who came 1st in the primary section may get addicted to drugs during their teenage. An extremely shy kid can become one of the well-known orator politicians in his youth. Who knows the future? Present is not equal to the future, so without making stories in the head, parents' dharma is to simply respond to the present moment with balance within and outside.

Parents are also the first gurus to their children, introducing them to this world and ways of living. It's the utmost duty and responsibility of a parent to first learn all that themselves. Know what it means to be a human and how to make the best out of it from being healthy to being abundant to being a contributor in this world. How to work with our body, mind, and breath. How to value one's life and how to be grateful for things like food on the plate to being alive in the moment, to fresh air and water. Giving birth to a life, upbringing should first start with learning about a human life, own life. Isn't it?

Besides, until the age of seven years, children are highly receptive. The emotional energy of parents is what they absorb. They learn to love, laugh, cry, worry, or get angry with the people around them. They learn the meaning of life and how to respond to life events by seeing how their early caregivers respond to life. Imagine how important it becomes for the parents (caregivers) to be fully conscious of their words, actions and reactions so that they can pass only the right impressions to the children. I learned this pretty late in life, but I sincerely hope that you, as a to-be parent or new parent, become aware and make the conscious choice of what you want to pass on to your children.

Not just parents, all elders, including teachers, have a similar role to play in a child's life and that is to become conscious of their words, responses and teachings. How I wish I had the awareness to be a more conscious parent when my child was born.

3.2c Dharma towards our parents

Parents who give birth to us, who bring us up with love and care, also need the same love and care in return. There may be disagreements, but love and dignity should never be lost in any action or interaction as children owe parents and ancestors a debt of gratitude for contributing to the gene pool as per scriptures.

Yes, there are all kinds of extreme cases in the world. Extreme parents to extreme children, however, the dharma of anyone is to do his/her part well. How do you do that is left to you because that is defined by your heart? Listen to it and do whatever makes you feel good from within. In most cases, the answer is to treat parents similarly as one would like to be treated by his/her own children.

3.2d Dharma towards our Teachers

Apart from love, knowledge & wisdom hold the highest value in a human life. Learning is the biggest gift one can give to oneself as wisdom dissolves all suffering. One can filter what to absorb and what to discard once there is wisdom and awareness.

As teachers play an important role in our lives after parents, we owe them huge gratitude. Teachers have to be treated with respect and dignity all throughout their lives. From school teachers to yoga teachers to guitar teacher to your mother, who teaches you to cook. Every knowledge is valuable and so is the person imparting that knowledge. Choosing to obey and follow anything or anyone is one's choice, but first listening to them with full attention itself is a mark of respect.

In present times, most students don't even know what respect means. Making fun of teachers, calling them names is supposedly a cool thing. Not paying attention and disturbing others is also supposedly a cool thing. It's not.

Teachers have changed life trajectories for ages and they continue to do so. We need gurus, mentors, and teachers at all times in our lives. We are here to learn till the end.

3.2e Dharma towards fellow human beings and society

We are all connected whether we agree or not just that unless things like covid come into our lives, we choose to be busy in our respective rat races and do not acknowledge how our actions and reactions are interconnected. We neither can survive alone nor be happy limiting our love and care just to ourselves and our immediate families.

The hero helps others… in movies and in reality. We love to see when a deserving child from a poor background comes up in life and fulfils his/her dreams and equally feel bad to see the injustice in society at many levels.

Goodness touches everyone and even the smallest of the effort makes a big difference. Service to humanity is considered service to God within us because it gives us joy. Hence, even our scriptures say we all must help the poor and the needy, the weak and the disabled because that way we help ourselves, we expand our love and joy.

Most importantly, power and strength come with responsibility and while it's absolutely necessary to help others in need, the least one can do is to never use the power over the weak & vulnerable (Physically, financially or mentally weak) including children, old people, physically challenged, mentally challenged or financially challenged.

Most people tend to show their anger and frustration only in front of the weak and vulnerable but choose to respond quite consciously in front of the strong. Example - Many people find it easy to show the power on small children at home, but find it difficult to utter a word before the senior at work as if elders have the right to be wrong but children have to be perfect.

The weaker the person we deal with, the more loving and caring our response needs to be.

3.2f Dharma towards other beings

Animals are vulnerable. Plants are vulnerable. As human brain is more evolved, other beings become vulnerable in front of us and so we have a higher responsibility and obligation to show compassion towards all living beings, practice non-violence, and avoid harming and hurting anyone, except in case of self-defence.

It is our responsibility as a human being to nourish the plants and animals within the available means and help them survive and flourish.

However, what have we been doing till now? Killing animals and destroying forests due to our greed. We are going against nature, against being a human being. A human being can't destroy the nature of which it is a part. Killing other beings is going against nature, going against the law of nature. (Nature doesn't mean things outside of us. Nature means the whole creation of which we are a part. We co-exist with everything else)

How would it be if a new species is born on earth with more evolved brains and starts eating human beings and destroying the ecosystem necessary for human survival? Difficult to imagine?

When it's difficult to tolerate injustice in our own lives, how can we be unjust to other beings? How can we be cruel to others? Before expecting God from heaven to set everything right in our lives, we should start acting like God when treating others, at least not kill or destroy. (By God here, I mean the perfect being we all want to exist in our lives and make everything perfect).

3.3 DHARMA TOWARDS ENVIRONMENT

Don't switch off the lights when going out, waste water as much as you want, use car AC full time even when not needed, and keep the car engine on even when it needs to be switched off. These are unlimited resources in our minds and things to be taken for granted. Right?

Unless the water bill or electricity bill or petrol bill is a thing of concern in the family, who cares? We hardly learn in our schools or at home how to save and value our resources.

Besides, we care only for our home and family. Someone in USA or Europe may not switch off his home lights thinking of the electricity shortage in India. New Zealand may not stop animal farming thinking of water scarcity in Africa. Forget about other continents or countries. Someone staying in Bangalore, India, may use as much amount of water or rather waste, as can be used to fulfil the needs of three people staying in villages nearby. There is enough for everyone's needs on earth but not for greed.

Wish there was one chapter on saving, valuing, and sharing what we have as humans in every school and religious book.

Everything around us, from water to air to plants, is necessary for our survival and they are limited. The quality and availability of all these depend on our actions. They are more expensive and precious than the paper money that we value so much. While we have been acting penny-wise and pound foolish for long, we have an obligation; we have dharma to protect our environment, to save our resources not just for our survival but for the survival of other beings too.

Our dharma towards the environment: No wastage of food or water starts from each home, restaurant, hotel, food chain and grocery store. One of the wildlife resorts near Bangalore takes a fine for wasting food on the plate. It's such a good practice. There people take only as much as they can finish and elders make sure to keep a check on children. This should be applied everywhere so that there is justice for those who don't get food. Similarly, water wastage can be avoided in many ways from closing the tap each time when not in use.

No wastage of electricity–Use only what you need at the time you need. Not necessary to switch on every room light at night. Not necessary to leave lights on when going out of the home.

No wastage of Petrol, Diesel or Gas–Walk or cycle wherever possible. Switch off the engine every time you can. Learn to live without AC unless absolutely necessary.

Planting minimum no of trees in our lifetime–No scripture mentions as a rule to plant any minimum no of trees during our lifetime. Still, I believe we should make our own rules just like no of books to be read in a year, we can individually decide on several trees/plants to grow and take care of them in our lifetime. If each one of us starts doing so since childhood as a law, we would contribute so much towards the environment. If there is enough green cover, soil will be protected, water resources will be protected, and various species will be protected. Our physical and mental health will be protected. How about planting at least one plant every year?

Choosing the natural way of living–By using the least amount of chemicals and non-disposable products in our own lives, and choosing natural products (from food to cosmetics to detergents), we can do our bit to protect the environment and ourselves in turn.

3.4 CLEANLINESS

Another most important dharma. Very basic but hardly followed, though we have been told many times cleanliness is next to godliness. We need cleanliness within as well as outside in our environment.

- No throwing garbage on roads or parks or beaches
- No throwing garbage or waste stuff into the rivers, lakes, ponds, oceans, etc

It's not that we do not pay a fine, the nature fines us itself for all wastages we do, for all the garbage we create and dispose of inappropriately. Those fines are natural disasters and they would keep increasing and become scarier if we don't start with every possible step at our level to start valuing what we have, to start saving what we have, and to start keeping our environment clean.

Look at ourselves as a part of creation. Whatever inputs we take in our bodies, there is a proper excretory system, and every waste goes out of our body in such a way that either it is completely used by the environment or gets decomposed. Co2 is used by plants, the shit turns into manure and our bodies post-death get automatically decomposed by the organism in the soil. All of our creations and industries also need such a rock-solid plan. We need to think of disposing of outputs properly first before even permitting any creation. No city, no village, no town, no apartment, no industry should be permitted until the planning is based on saving what we have and disposing of what we don't need most appropriately.

Decluttering- Clarity of mind is our responsibility and clarity comes in a clean environment. Our home, our office space, is our vision board. Our mind gets messages all the time from our surroundings. What one can do.

- Everything has a place and everything is in place–Structure helps. Everything needs to have a designated place in our surroundings. Labelling, separate sections, and files bring structure.
- Doing your bit everyday day - Small steps of keeping things in place daily can save one from loads of work.
- Don't' keep what you don't need- Whatever is not needed either give to charity or dispose of properly. Old stuff at home, old stuff in mind.
- Declutter once a week–From home to office to closet to your personal table.
- Once a year - Deep cleaning. Diwali as a festival also is meant for the same purpose

3.5 MORAL DUTIES

This comes exactly as mentioned in the scriptures. Every human being must practice virtues to live righteously and cultivate purity (sattva), and discernment (buddhi). These include praying, self-restraint, discipline, resolve, good works, and the practice of nonviolence, truthfulness, non-stealing, and non-covetousness. Other duties include respecting the elders, parents and teachers, taking care of old and aged members of the family, helping children to grow up, and avoiding the cardinal sins, namely lust, anger, pride, envy, and delusion.

We have come very far from all these virtues and practices, yet we need to remind ourselves of these values time and again because purity and discernment are what we need to achieve higher states (mentally and spiritually)

We have come very far from all these virtues and practices, yet we need to remind ourselves of these values time and again because purity and discernment are what we need to achieve higher states (mentally and spiritually)

3.6 PROFESSIONAL DUTIES

3.6a - Our scriptures say, those in the leadership position or senior position have to act fairly and impartially without falling for temptations and selfishness.

Doesn't happen this way, right? We all like to favour those we like when compared to those who make us feel insecure due to their superior qualities or those who don't behave the way we want them to, even if they are deserving. Politics from the business world to government is one of the worst diseases of modern society. Very few realize that seniority at work too comes with the responsibility of being fair and unbiased. They also create Karma.

Our simple act of giving to non- deserving instead of giving the due to the deserving can have a cascading effect. Effect on the immediate family to the employee's mental health to society the organization as a whole to the whole world. The reason we have extremism everywhere.

Besides, taking advantage of the situation or someone's position in the name of policies and rules is also a myopic way of seeing life. As the world is round, life is also a circle. What goes around does come around just that from our relative position, we can't see the entire picture immediately. The point is we understand each other by energy, so no matter how smartly the boss plays politics by placing the gun on someone else's shoulder, the intentions become evident eventually. And the fact is, we are all connected. If the action is filtering from one's dharma, the action is bound to be there and will come back in some way or the other. Professionally being right in one's judgement and being just needs deliberate intention & practice, and we must be so.

If you want to grow, help others grow. If you want respect from seniors, give respect to your juniors. If you want to be heard, listen to others first. If you want justice, be just to others. If you want a fair deal, be fair to others. If you don't want to be taken advantage of, don't take undue advantage of others. If you want people to keep their words, you start keeping your words.

Words have weight. Don't just say things for the heck of it. Don't show anyone rosy pictures that you can't produce, …this applies primarily to the sophisticated corporate world & Government.

3.6 b–Spreading knowledge of Dharma (way of being) is the highest karma, and vice versa is also true. Worst karma is to spread hatred, violence, injustice, and wrong teachings in the name of dharma or religion. Anything that goes against humanity and nature can't be anyone's dharma.

As per the scriptures, all those who become spiritual teachers, or take up priesthood functions, have to live virtuously and spread the knowledge of the Dharma, which means love, compassion and laws of nature (humanity included).

All those who are misinterpreting dharma (duty as a human) or religion (a particular system of faith), fighting in the name of religion, suppressing others in the name of religion, and using religion for political or social advantage are doing the opposite.

Let's understand Dharma and religion–Dharma is one's duty or way of being in a specific context at a specific time. It is a way of being as human as we are and coexisting in this nature without harming any other being. Dharma is about good energy& intention. If we want to be loved, love becomes our dharma towards others. If we want justice, being just becomes our dharma towards others. Plants follow dharma, and animals follow dharma.

On the other hand, religion (system of faith) exists only in human societies. Religion is a set of rules and rituals either written or verbally communicated in various ways from time to time within societies depending on the level of awareness then. The teachings of any religion depend on the time of its birth and the conditions that prevailed in the society then. So, everything may or may not be relevant today. At least this much we all should be open to. Religions do need regular upgrades with human evolution. Human evolution means moving towards higher values that is pure love and wisdom.

Most importantly, while there are broad guidelines on dharma in various religions, no one can decide or has the right to decide the action for another person in a specific context in the name of dharma. Forcing anyone to follow anything is an absolute no-no. This creation has given the freewill/choice to the individual. Following anything, including dharma, is also one's choice. Nature has an inbuilt cause-and-effect system that takes care of all kinds of choices.

3.6 c Traders, merchants, and professionals (doctors, engineers etc) have to practice their professions without cheating and deception. While times are difficult and there are all kinds of customers, the least is not to cheat or deceive anyone.

A civil engineer needs to remember that his children and loved ones may end up using the roads, and the bridges built under him. Medical seat board committee should know that if they give the medical seat to an incapable person, tomorrow their loved one may become the victim of medical negligence. Cheating and deceiving others is cheating oneself.

3.6 d Finally, those who take up manual labour or are in junior positions should do their part in serving others, without expecting unnecessary support or freebies.

3.7 DHARMA TOWARDS OTHER FAITHS

As each individual is unique, so is his story and so is his path to evolution and total wisdom. We are all at different levels of awareness, wisdom, and mental evolution. With limited knowledge and experience, none of us can surely say which is the best faith system (religion) for all and hence we are expected to show restraint and friendliness in dealing with people of other faiths and live in harmony with them. Fanaticism and intolerance are completely ruled out because we can't teach someone not to hate by hating him. Our dharma gets violated that way.

Part 4

Our Rights

Irrespective of our birthplace, time, country, and environment, we all make choices every moment. The choice to accept, the choice to reject, the choice to change, the choice to take an action, the choice not to do anything, the choice to cry, the choice to smile, and so on. Free will or the right to choose is something that is given in human life. The choice here means how we respond to every life event.

Most importantly, **since the choice lies with us, the responsibility also lies with us because when we make a choice, we also choose the outcome or the consequence by default, whether we have the intuition to anticipate it or not. Our action as well as inaction is a choice.**

Getting it? The better the intuition, the better equipped one is to anticipate the outcome and decide accordingly.

However, before developing intuition and working with it, firstly, all of us have to know that we have a choice in every situation and in some cases, we have specific rights.

The surprising part is most people who are suppressed or abused don't even know that they have a right to make a choice, to make a change, to not accept. They are never taught explicitly about their rights.

Whenever I heard about children getting abused at home or in school, I always thought of writing this book for them. Not just children… it is about all those who are weak in the society and in the world who are not fully aware of their power to choose. Many times, whatever is unfair or wrong happens, most people simply accept it because they think others have the right to be the way they are.

A small child who comes into this world, trying to figure things out, gets into a family where abuse is normal, and may simply accept it as part of parenting. No child exactly knows what to expect from parents or teachers or people around apart from what his/her instincts say.

Small children, women, physically weak, financially weak… the exploited list is long. So, here is an attempt to discuss the rights that we have as human beings.

Remember, choosing to be exploited is also bad karma, especially when you are at an age to understand it. Most people accept the wrong in the present due to the fear of the future. Past is gone, future is unknown. We all have a present. If the present is worse, why fear the future? First, take the action in the present. Who knows? You may create a better future than your present. We are unjust to ourselves when we accept any form of exploitation.

4.1 RIGHT TO FREEDOM

The most important right is the right to freedom. Freedom to live and make choices as long as one doesn't harm anyone, kill anyone, suppress anyone, or be unjust to anyone, including the self.

Every right comes with a responsibility, and so does the right of freedom. One individual's freedom shouldn't be another person's pain. While individuals have certain rights, they also have corresponding responsibilities to ensure that the exercise of those rights does not infringe upon the rights of others or harm the greater good of society.

The enjoyment of individual liberties should be balanced with a sense of responsibility to prevent harm to others or the broader community. In societies that value individual freedoms, legal and ethical frameworks often seek to establish boundaries to ensure that the exercise of rights does not lead to negative consequences for others.

Every word, every expression, and every action of ours influences and affects someone or the other on everyday basis and hence we all need to act wise, meaning think long term & understand the consequences first before acting our rights.

- Freedom of Expression–We have the freedom to express our thoughts, ideas, opinions and dreams in any form, including writing, art, cinema and speech
- Freedom of Speech–Each one of us has the right to speak for and against anything
- Assembly without arms–There is the freedom to assemble in groups without arms and ammunitions
- Freedom to join any association–We have the freedom to join or associate ourselves with any group of our choice except the groups which work against the society & spread hatred in anyway
- Freedom to practice any profession–Each one of us has the right to choose the career or profession that we wish to undertake, irrespective of what our ancestors did or our elders want us to do. There is no obligation to follow the family profession and no one can be forced to join any profession
- Residing in any part of the Country–Each person has the right to reside and settle in any part of the country

Right to freedom… yes, but what we do with that freedom creates our karma. The choice we make while exercising our rights creates our karma. And it's important that we become more conscious and careful before exercising any right.

4.2 RIGHT AGAINST EXPLOITATION

No one has the right to exploit anyone irrespective of age, gender, caste, creed, religion, professional position, or financial status. Nobody means nobody. Every being not just humans but animals & plants too need to be seen as equal shareholders of this creation and so no one is above the other.

Addressing every vulnerable section below to explicitly state their rights and what they can do about it.

Children: Please know that no elder, including parent, teacher, uncle and aunt, neighbour, etc has any right to hit or inappropriately touch you or abuse you in any other way. Even though you are small, you have the choice not to allow or accept abuse. Find someone you trust the most within the family or in school and always speak up.

You can yell, you can scream, you can immediately let people know when someone tries to do the wrong to save yourself. The one whose actions are inappropriate needs to be ashamed of what he/she does. As children, you shouldn't be ashamed of others' actions. You do not need to suffer.

What you can do further – First tell everything to that one person you can trust be it a parent or a teacher or a relative or sibling.

Beyond that **call child helpline in your country/city. For Indian children it is 1098 -Childline India foundation.**

Old parents: No one, including your own children, has any right to hit or abuse you. Society's image is not as important as your own self-esteem. Take help. You have the right to lead a dignified life. It's always better to stay alone than be with children who abuse you in any way.

What you can do–Inform other relatives who you trust. Use this helpline –

National elder helpline (by government) –

Tel: 14567, Operational Across India HELPAGE HELPLINE (By Helpage India NGO): 1800-180-1253 Operational in 21 states and DIGNITY HELPLINE (N.G.O) 18002678780 (Monday to Friday - 10 AM to 6 PM)

Cast: We are nature, we are governed by laws of nature. Society is created by us. The rules of every society are created by certain powerful groups and individuals from time to time who are limited by their awareness and experience. Just because something becomes popular or a way of life in society doesn't mean it is the right thing or it has to be followed. In fact, society is the worst mirror to see yourself in.

Am not saying everything in society is wrong, but please understand that just because something is done by 100 people, it may not be the right thing to do. Social trends keep changing with time and exposure. They are not always born out of wisdom gained over time. The most important thing is to use judgement and understand your own good and the good of others, irrespective of who stands with you.

Professional Position: No one has the right to exploit the other person due to his/her professional position. Yet this happens & is one of the most prevalent forms of injustice and unfairness in our society. Whether it is the government or corporate world, police or army, certain individuals and groups not only take undue advantage of their position but also become blind due to the power in their hands.

Many deserving candidates are left behind for not being in the right place among the right people, and this is one of the most common forms of suffering in the professional world today. Apart from hindering growth, there is exploitation & harassment at many levels, primarily mental, but in some cases physical too.

Such things exist because someone else doesn't know his worth. This exists because someone somewhere doesn't believe in himself/herself about what he/she can do. The burden of responsibilities always seems bigger than the belief in oneself to be able to take risks.

Most people don't realize that by tolerating injustice and unfair treatment, they pay much higher costs for what they receive in terms of remuneration or post. We all have the right to make a different choice, even in such situations.

Right to act, right to change the job, right to vote to change the government, right to join politics ourselves, etc. If one's own mindset is a problem, a belief system is a problem, then working with the mindset is a choice. Finding solutions or tolerating the wrong are two different choices.

Financial Status: We all know there is a huge gap and disparity in our societies in terms of the distribution of wealth and this gap has been increasing. With technology, increasing exposure and easy access to various things, life is becoming more difficult for have-nots.

Over and above, if there is exploitation or ill-treatment by the rich towards the poor, it is an extremely sad situation. Power, position and riches should make one humble, respectful & caring towards others. How we treat people on the road, how we treat people at restaurants, how we treat people within the family, every single interaction counts.

All those who look down upon themselves and look up at others due to financial status just know that wealth & money doesn't give any right to anyone to misbehave or mistreat. No one can do so unless you allow the same.

First thing, do not forget to respect yourself, don't keep your eyes down. Money and wealth is not equal to how great a person is. Greatness of a person is not defined by the means he has but the qualities he develops. Get inspired by others, but don't look up to someone because that way, you would look down upon yourself. Treat yourself equal to everyone else.

4.3 RIGHT TO FREEDOM OF RELIGION

Each individual on earth has the choice to follow any religion, any belief system irrespective of the birth and can even change the religion in due course of life. Yes, some countries, some states, and some societies do not allow this, but in most developed countries and developing nations like India, the constitution gives the right to freedom of religion.

Most of the times, religions become merely a set of rituals and rules one is supposed to follow. There is no understanding or questioning the system. The important thing is the intention with which any religion is born and how relevant it is in today's context.

Rules and rituals do make sense in uncivilized, unscrupulous societies where there is no direction. It is basically to divert human energies towards something and keep them busy. And there can be various ways to do it hence exist many religions across the world. However, they may or may not lead to the exploration of human nature and life, which is the main purpose. Yet so many wars have been fought and are still on in the name of religion. Not worth it, right?

Beliefs shouldn't be forced upon because of birth or marriage or anything else. Beliefs should be questioned all the time and must be upgraded with new learnings.

Religion is such a sensitive topic across the world that I would only suggest, 'Be who you want to be inside, follow things your heart agrees to and relates to irrespective of the religion you are supposed to follow outside because of birth'. Even fighting for your beliefs with the outside world is a waste of time.

Connecting to God, Bhagwan, or Allah is very personal. There is no one way to connect to the creator. The way every human being is different, ways of connecting to God are bound to be different, too. So, you can be anyone from outside- Hindu, Muslim, Buddhist, Jewish etc, doesn't matter. What you choose inside matters from time to time with your evolution and awareness.

And human evolution means moving towards pure love and wisdom. Pure love and wisdom are not known as Hindu, Muslim, or anything. The day we start discarding every politician, every journalist, and every teacher who uses the name of religion to talk about disparity, unfairness, crimes, and injustice, we will resolve most conflicts that exist today.

4.4 CULTURAL AND EDUCATIONAL RIGHTS

These rights aim to ensure that individuals and communities have the freedom to preserve, develop, and express their cultural identities and participate fully in educational opportunities without discrimination. Which means, you can do the following freely

Preserve and Promote your Culture: You can preserve, develop, and express your cultural identity, language, traditions, and customs. This includes the right to maintain and practice cultural rituals, ceremonies, and traditions, as well as the protection of cultural heritage sites linked to you.

Use your own language - Language is a big part of who we are. You have the right to use, preserve, and promote your native language in education, public services, media, and other domains. This includes the right to receive education in one's own language and to have official documents and services available in minority languages.

Access to Education: Educational rights ensure that everyone has access to quality education without discrimination. This includes access to primary, secondary, and higher education, as well as vocational and adult education programs. Governments are typically tasked with providing free and compulsory education up to a certain age and ensuring equal opportunities for all, regardless of gender, race, ethnicity, religion, or socioeconomic status.

Freedom of Thought and Expression: Cultural and educational rights often intersect with freedom of thought, conscience, and expression. As an individual you are free to share your cultural beliefs and ideas without worrying about being stopped or punished. This also means having the freedom to learn about different cultures and take part in cultural activities.

Protecting Indigenous Peoples: Indigenous groups have special cultural and educational rights to protect their unique cultures, languages, and knowledge. These rights help them control their own education and keep their traditions alive.

4.5 RIGHT TO CONSTITUTIONAL REMEDIES

Most importantly know that you have the right to seek legal remedies or solutions from courts if your fundamental rights guaranteed by the constitution of your country are violated by the government individual or any authority.

Even if it takes long to get justice in most cases especially in developing nations, seek it in first place.

Part 5

Happiness–What drives us

The simplest and the most complicated word in today's world.

- In Indian movies they show happiness as the heroine getting drunk, feeling high, dancing on the road, the hero getting excited with the personality change, thinking about what's coming. Society starts associating happiness with booze, with dancing and singing, with merrymaking, with certain expressions.
- Others spend years meditating in the name of happiness to experience the desired mental states. Monks and Sages. Years of meditation! Some of them even leave their homes and families in search of happiness. That's the complicated part. The girl above seems smarter here.
- The third category is about the online & offline gurus selling happiness formulae nowadays. Mostly associated with boosting one's hope for getting things one wants. That's more complicated. The never-ending cycle of wants.
- Then there is this social media. The fact that we have to look happy and high in life has added pressure and competition in every aspect of our lives–beauty, travel, partying, lifestyles, friendships, and even charity. We are proving everything all the time. We are declaring that we are happy and high, even via WhatsApp and Facebook status updates.

Of course, being happy and high is a necessity because then only people flock around you or look up to you irrespective of what's true in your life. In fact, if your life sucks at a certain stage but you show your cheerful face outside, it is considered a sign of strength. This, I feel, is the most complicated part because what we show outside has taken precedence over what we truly & authentically feel inside. Not an advocate of spreading negativity, but when we lie to ourselves, we lose touch with reality and the present.

Action towards good happens when acknowledgement towards not good feelings is there. Good, here as in the meaning of good in our heads. We are the ones who give meaning to the events and happenings throughout our lives.

For instance, we have so trained ourselves with social norms & trends and the meanings & symbols we learn throughout our lives, that we mostly assume a smiling face, a humorous person, a wealthy entrepreneur means a happy person.

Likewise, someone who is not popular among friends or doesn't join parties could be boring for many. However, things are not as simple as they seem.

We have layers of feelings. Some we know, some we don't even know. Yes, if one smiles, dances or exercises, the physicality supports mental status. However, for authentic joy, all the hidden layers of emotions also need to be addressed. The mind needs to be addressed. And, the understanding has to come from within. It's like getting into the mind to sort the stuff in mind with our own reasoning and understanding.

Coming back to happiness. What makes one happy differs for each one of us. Besides the fact that, in our own lives, the definition or meaning of happiness is bound to change and will change with time and our growing up.

Art of happiness, I am still figuring out like everyone else. Science of happiness, yes! We can learn that here. There is research done based on brain scans to study the mental states of different people. And It looks like…

Happiness is as much physical (release of chemicals) as it is mental (thinking, feeling, choosing).

Going back to the thinking - feeling - choosing cycle of our lives. I repeat, thinking creates feeling and feeling generates energy. Energy in motion is emotion.

Every feeling corresponds to a specific chemical in our body. Different emotions trigger the synthesis of different molecules in the brain. For instance, happiness leads to the release of pleasure molecules like dopamine, while stress or panic induces the production of cortisol. The state of bliss is prolonged happiness (the forever happy state). It's the highest state that higher beings achieve through various practices.

There are seven pleasure molecules that create elevated mental states or "happy highs" or the flow. Each pleasure molecule serves a unique purpose:

Dopamine motivates us, whether through achieving goals, indulging in treats, or experiencing luxury. Your favourite ice cream in front of you... you craving & receiving it, that's dopamine. You expecting promotion and getting it, that's Dopamine.

Oxytocin creates warmth and connection, often released during hugs or meaningful social interactions. Our social lives, meeting with an old close friend, give a boost to our oxytocin levels

Norepinephrine boosts alertness and excitement, such as during thrilling activities like watching sports or favourite movie with your friends.

Serotonin provides satisfaction and a sense of connection, like when being with loved ones or in serene environments like a jungle or waterfront.

Nitric Acid enhances intensity, particularly during workouts, by widening blood vessels and increasing circulation.

Beta Endorphin induces body ecstasy, felt after exercise or sexual activity.

Anandamide, the bliss molecule, produces a state of flow and timelessness during enjoyable activities like painting, writing or creating anything that needs full attention.

So now we know how to be happy scientifically. You need dopamine. Get promoted every year. Not possible? Start having more of the ice creams you like. 😊

Most of the above examples are dependent on external things which are not in our control. And even if some of them are, it won't help for long enough. Law of marginal utility says with every increase in the amount of ice creams in your life there will be a comparatively lesser increase in dopamine release. You will want more and more of ice cream or alcohol or anything else that gives you a high, leading to health issues. Besides, the need for ice cream will be directly proportional to the demotivation in your personal and professional lives.

And Creation doesn't allow greed or any form of extremes to get away without punishment at any level. Of course, there is a time lag between cause and effect so that we humans get enough chances to make the right choice.

Moreover, anything that gives a sudden high will also give a sudden low once removed, just like a seesaw. Reason alcohol and drugs are associated with bipolar disorders.

Any extreme is bad- We can't keep eating fatty, sugary food for dopamine, we can't keep watching sports while sitting with friends all the time for norepinephrine, and we can't always keep running away from the present to people and places for feeling connected and of course, we can't go to extremes for body ecstasy. Even too much exercise can be bad at times.

On the other hand, who needs momentary happiness, we want happiness to last longer. In fact, why not all the time? So, we need to know both ways to release dopamine. One by eating ice cream (If ice cream means happiness in our head) and another without eating ice cream too. So on and so forth. Balance is the key demand by nature so our dependence on external can't go overboard.

This is where we use various mind practices to mentally get to the feel good states irrespective of external reality or else anyone who is feeling demotivated at work or home will end up compensating that with addictions either for food (sugars & fats) or alcohol or drugs or good times unless the person takes over the mind.

The choice to work with our minds or to blindly follow addictions for the release of happy hormones lies with us. Sacrificing short-term happiness for the long-term good is a better judgment any day.

This much we all have experienced may not have acknowledged, though.

Happiness is a skill; it is a practice; it is choosing habits& thoughts that support our long-term well-being; it is something that needs to be learnt and grasped internally.

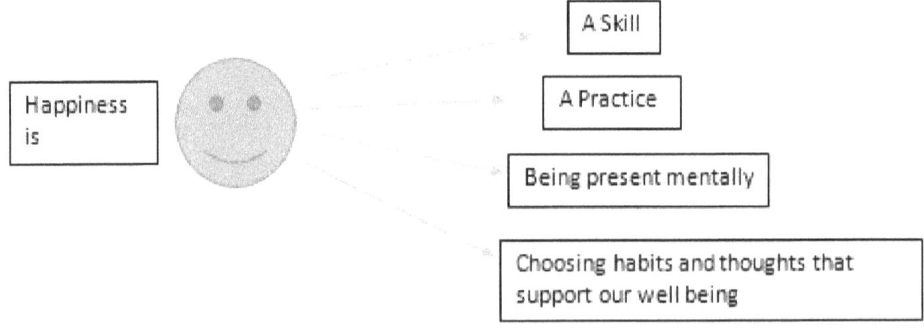

When people say happiness is a choice, they don't mean you dig a pit to bury your feelings and show something else outside. It means one needs to internalize the practice of being present, one needs to work with one's mind (thoughts) and habits that support one's wellbeing. Authentically feeling fine or ok with whoever we are and wherever we are.

Working with the mind is an effort and requires the continuous practice of bringing oneself to the present moment. Let's understand the why and how part of this.

Mind, brain and happy feeling

Because of our minds, we have developed a natural tendency to slip into a state of unhappiness and chaos. As per the research works on the brain, if we look at the brain scans even during no physical activity, in most cases it looks like a fish market. Stressed, confused, and overworked. The result is not feeling good or unhappy.

The point is, even in the state of physical rest, our brains are super active. Why? Because our minds are misusing, exploiting our brains, loading them with overthinking & unnecessary work. We are not present or focused most of the time, busy in all kinds of races and to-dos based on the good or bad meanings in our minds.

Focus or being present in the present is a mandate to feel relaxed, composed and mentally fine. This is the art of happiness, which will vary from person to person. Below is my recipe.

Developing attention or focus: –These are some of the things that I have tried. You have the choice to make your own list and do trial and error until you arrive at whatever makes you feel it's the path for you.

1. **Novelty:** When we fall in love for the first time or when we experience something new and interesting, our mind pays attention. On the other hand, anything that becomes part of daily chores, including driving on the same route every time, you would see that your mind has the tendency to drift away very easily and you get lost in the thoughts. So, trying new things and experiences helps to keep novelty factor alive in life and so the attention. Don't mean falling in love every day with a different girl. In the same relationship, novelty can be brought in by learning new things together, doing different activities together, even by traveling and exploring new places together.
2. **Thrill:** During adventure sports such as mountain climbing, deep sea diving, bungee jumping etc. where there is a fear of fall or injury, focus comes naturally. Here, we choose to pay full attention to be careful. Since the brain is not used to of the task, it pays attention to the task. This is a great way to meditate. Meditation is not just sitting with closed eyes. All these activities are meditations for many of us. Besides, throughout the day, whenever there is a gap between thoughts and we pay full attention to the moment, it is meditating.
3. **Building or creating things one loves:** When we get to the task of creating new, building something new obviously, we need all attention for creative juices to flow. Not everyone gets a job he/she loves or the big idea of making a living out of entrepreneurship. Doesn't matter. Building and creating you love doesn't have to be your paid job. Some things should be done just for ourselves and for the sake of our mental well-being. Build for yourself and create for yourself just to focus and pay attention in a good way. Creativity demands attention.

4. **Harmonious Relationships:** As per the longest study on happiness by Harvard where they have studied the lives of 724 men for over 75 years, one of the major factors that increases the happiness quotient in life is relationships. Happiness of a human being is a lot dependent on the relationships, social circle and community. The more social connections we have, not virtual, the chances of being happier and healthier are more. So, this is clue. If nothing else is working fine in our heads, we can always stick to family or friends or both depending on what works. This is also one area where most of our lessons come from.
5. **The art of doing nothing:** Lastly, it pays to practice sitting with oneself doing nothing, literally doing nothing but simply observing. Imagine yourself running from left to right all the time, left being the past and right being the future. Obviously, this continuous run would make anyone tired, the reason we usually experience fatigue. And that's why we need to sit in one place that is present and just observe everything from our position without running.

6. **Conscious living:** Being conscious of where our thoughts take us throughout the day. I remind myself as much as possible to keep a check if I am mentally present in a specific place or not and try to bring myself back again to the moment. It's not easy for sure. There is so much junk inside. There was a time

when I used to be proud of the fact that I had strong likes and dislikes. Today, I know the culprit of all wanderings. And this knowing is not enough. The reminder I need is to continue with practice.

I need to practice that nothing has meaning unless I give it the same. If I don't conclude any life event as bad in my head, I won't need any outside help. Bad exists because there are things in my head that mean good. Declaring something good and bad leads to endless thinking either about the past or the future. Duality (Good and bad) exists in the mind, reality is neutral. And trust me am equally attached to the meanings in my mind. My desires haven't ended. I still have a long list that keeps getting updated with the challenges life throws at me

My understanding is that we learn and continue to learn the meanings of happiness partly from society and trends & partly from our perceptions. Nothing is good or bad whether earning more money is happiness in your head or dancing like a mad in the pub. Only thing is we must remind ourselves not to conclude the meaning of happiness for ourselves or others and start judging. Today, being Falguni Nayar could mean happiness in our minds. Tomorrow it could be a hippie. So, when the destination happiness is not constant in our heads, it's a wild goose chase to keep running for things one after another. Isn't it?

Besides, is there any other option than to make peace with whoever we are, wherever we are in this moment, to give some rest to our minds?

Also, while it's still ok to enjoy this never-ending wild goose chase in our own lives if we all choose to do, the bigger problem starts when we start defining happiness (Career, position, power, etc) for our kids too and start concluding. Follow the next chapter for more.

Part 6

Being a Parent–Why and How to Start on a Good Note

I had to write about this because this topic is the closest to my heart. We need to correct things from the start even before we decide to become parents. Parenting is the most important role we play in our lives. It's a foundation of humanity, the root of all things we see around in our society.

I so wish I had known all this, what I am going to write here before. Children have been my biggest weakness. For years, my everyday prayer has been 'All the children in this world are healthy, happy, and safe at all times'. Ironically, I had even written a blog on my ideologies of how children should be treated, before becoming a parent.

Yet I faltered as a parent during testing times because the lessons I was avoiding to learn otherwise were meant to come out of my parenting challenges. God chose my son to be one of my teachers in life. I read books; I did a course to learn parenting; I took out 10 days to learn Vipassana meditation to get some clue as to why was I struggling so much with my teenager.

It took me quite some time to understand my lessons. I did learn a few of those the hard ways, but I know I still have a long way to go.

Experience is indeed the best teacher. We all prefer to make all mistakes ourselves and learn, still, I am attempting to put forth certain ideas in front of you because the stakes are very high here. Parenting mistakes are too heavy to be carried in our hearts and children are too precious to be mistreated. Parenting is not natural as we have understood till now, it needs to be learnt.

I hope that you acknowledge that giving birth to a life is one of the greatest gifts and the cost of starting on the wrong note is too high here not just for one life but for the whole of humanity. So let me share what I can.

Like most parents, 'I had just this one idea in my head. I want my son's good.'

Nothing wrong with this, right? But I failed to understand two things.

- What is meant by my child's good?
- How can I be truly loving to my child to ensure his well-being?

I learnt that

1. Parenting is not about raising or fixing the child, it is about raising ourselves, fixing ourselves. The best gift that we can give to our children is our continued improvement in the way we respond to life events. A loving parent works on himself/herself too.

   A loving parent is not equal to a pampering parent, or the one who gives everything that the child asks for. A loving parent is equal to the one who works on his continued awakening.

2. We are not supposed to ever stop trying to guide children or help them pursue the right direction as far as we know, however, no force, no anxiousness, no deciding on their behalf, and no inflicting pain for non-obedience. Parenting demands hard work. Just because children are small and weak, inflicting pain in any form (screaming, spanking, shaming, scaring, etc.) to get things done seems the easiest way for parents. We never go and hit our bosses, or our politicians or express anger at our mother-in-law so anger is a choice, trust me. Not a reflex. It happens only because the strong dominate the weak.

3. There is too much power in the hands of parents as against the young child. Parents can do anything- yell, hit, shame them, but with any power comes responsibility. Huge responsibility.

4. In most struggles, it is the problem of acceptance. We don't want to accept what we don't like. Children don't listen or follow because they don't want to accept what they don't like. We react, we resist, and our children learn from us the way to respond to life when one doesn't like something. They learn non-acceptance of the reality from us. They learn to react and not the way to respond or act in a given situation. Reactions could simply be pain, or disappointment (expressed or unexpressed) resulting in sulking, yelling, hitting, verbal abuse, shaming, punishing etc.

   We project anxious energies all the time and that gets absorbed by them. We are anxious about their health, their education, their safety, their morality, their not going to school, their throwing or wasting the food, their spending hours in front of the screen. So on and so forth.

   We are always struggling to ensure that we get only what we like in life, especially when it comes to our children. Life gives all kinds of results, at least it feels that way till the time we have a list of likes and dislikes/ good and bad.

   It's not that if our children are at some risk due to wrong exposure, we would simply say yes to continue. We need to act; we need to respond, but this anxiousness and mindless reaction has to go. And first from our end.

   Point to note: I would have at least cried a hundred times while dealing with my son and I still do at times behind closed doors. I have left home, taken multiple breaks, felt like, 'I should never have been his mother or I should not have been in his life' on multiple occasions, yet am here with the opposite idea that parents need to work on themselves while guiding the children.

5. My child's good doesn't mean that to ensure his good or well-being, I would go down as far as my thinking, feeling and acting patterns are concerned. I must only ensure my response to life is appropriate and gets better with time. That is the best that I can do for my child. This is ensuring good from my end. We don't have control over others and their destiny, including the destiny of our children. We can't control our child's destiny. We are only supposed to do our part well by being conscious of every thought, feeling, and action.
6. The fact is, we can't always protect our children from not experiencing things we don't like or they don't like. They are bound to be unhappy if getting everything that one want or likes is happiness. The only thing we can teach them is how to take what happens in life. And that too, not in words. We teach children how to respond to life through our real-time responses to life events, including when our children do things, we don't like at all and that may include our worst parenting nightmares thanks to online exposure.
7. Most of us grow up with the idea that we have to be happy and successful. The meaning of happiness and success is concluded based on our personal experience, our past, society and social trends. And we start seeing our children through the same lens. They too learn their meanings depending on the exposure they get. Even if parents don't define it for them, media, school, friends, etc do the job for them.

Happiness & success is a myth in the sense that, it is a mindless run by our present social standards not just in terms of money, fame, position, good times but also a run for anything which we are not including a good boy or a good girl.

Not sure at what point one can feel successful enough or happy enough. While we would all want our children to look happy, do we know where exactly lies their happiness if we remove references from social examples, memories and past data? Our own destination happiness keeps moving, right?

So, if we leave the meaning of happiness and success to our child and on time, let's list down what we have control on:

1. We only have control in doing our part right. That is the way we choose to respond irrespective of what happens, because that's a moment of real teaching to our children. And most importantly setting the intention right matters. Once we decide or put a serious intention to do our part right rather than fix what's wrong in our child, things are bound to fall into place with time.
2. Our job as parents is not to make them doctors, engineers, Amitabh Bachchans, Sachin Tendulkars or Ambanis, our job is primarily to teach them how to take life, how to take care of themselves and how to manage themselves, their emotions by being an example. That's a choice we have.
3. We have the choice to be a good example; learn& improve our own emotions handling. How? You can do your own trial and error and arrive at which method you like& can do. I can list some of them here, like meditation, journaling, and everyday practice, to train the brain for dealing with anxieties and fears. Constant reminders to your own self. Choosing the right habits for yourself. Working on every aspect of your lives by treating yourself as a whole. Read inspiring books, listen to inspiring people, and join supportive communities. Meditation can be learned, changing habits can be learned, and brain training can

be learned. This is not out of course syllabus. Everything can be learnt. Just that learning should become a priority to overcome challenges.

4. We have the choice to bless ourselves and our children every day.
5. We have the choice to give them the right environment, from a loving home to education, to our quality time and attention.
6. Last but not the least, we as parents have the choice to align ourselves first. Learn parenting together. Decide to give a one common message to the child for the child's long term good. Two different messages on anything may just lead to confusion for the child and then they won't know what to do. We have learnt the hard way here.

Things I feel were right actions on my part

1. Blessing my child every night while putting him to sleep, and I continue to do that. My blessing has been like a prayer for his well-being, which he heard every day just before sleeping when the brain is in the alpha state of mind.
2. Reading to my child at night. This is the time I would even read books with great ideas or messages that I wanted to pass on to him.
3. Treating him as equal when it came to any important decision. He was fully involved in all decision makings especially when it came to his life choices. For ex, he chose all his schools. We always did trials before joining any school or class.
4. Giving him a lot of exposure. Would send him everywhere to do things on his own, from buying to banking to traveling.
5. I had read that till the age of 8 years, whatever the child sees and hears becomes part of his permanent memory, so I never

tried to scare my child, even in the name of ghost or anything. I never said weather change could make him sick. Instead, I said his body knows to heal itself.

Please make your own list and see what has worked well and share with others too.

Points to remember

- Discipline is always self-discipline. So, we as parents need to create our inner boundaries first. For ex, if I want my child to sleep by 10 pm, I need to switch off all screens, including my phone and Wi-Fi by 10 pm consistently at home. There will always be exceptions. Parents can be very disciplined themselves and the child may be the opposite or the child could be very sincere as opposed to his/her parents. That's ok. What we get is not in our hands. What we do is.
- Parents can't go down their level(thinking/feeling/acting) to improve the child's level, that way the whole purpose is lost. Aversion and craving both lead to disaster. Craving towards a child's great future and aversion towards what is the reality. Both generate extreme emotions and anxiety. Right actions are taken in calm.
- Parenting is a cleaning process, a deep cleaning process for ourselves. A test to refine the human within us. Many of my worst moments when I have broken down, given up, lost my senses then again got myself back to track have been part of my learning as a parent and it goes on. We don't become right or balanced in just one stroke.
- We communicate through energies and feelings, not through words with our children. The day you are down, your child will give you a harder time

- Whatever is told to the child, in front of the child and whatever he sees and experiences till 8 years of his age, becomes a part of his permanent memory. This includes the energy we project.
- Child's good lies in parents getting better and better in their response to life events. Managing their thinking, feeling, and acting part well. Managing & processing their own emotions well. Doing the inner work, raising the child within first.
- When nature has given free will to everyone including us and there is a cause-and-effect mechanism in place, we as parents also must respect both free will and natural cause-and-effect mechanisms. Whatever we can change, we can. We necessarily must stop at the point when it becomes a force. The parenting journey is a lot of hard work, a lot of patience, and a lot of surrender & trust towards the nature of life. Forcing can be bad to the extent that when an infant who is force-fed all the time can even grow up to be a child accepting abuse as normal. Anything by force is a usual event in life that should never happen. Free will is for all. We can try our best to convince children, but no forcing, no blackmailing.
- The suffering on the parents' part is not because of the number of times they have to say anything or explain anything. It comes from the anxiety and hopelessness, the emotions that we attach to reality because of not getting what we expect. I feel terrible when I am helpless. And this is exactly where the inner work is needed. It's not easy on behalf of parents to see even basic minimal things not done at times. And that's why precisely, it requires huge strength building to accept what seems abnormal and unfair at times.
- There are no quick-fix solutions to situations. Each child is different so the parenting challenge and the right thing to do in a specific context is directly proportional to the wisdom within.

As parents we need to learn, grow and improve in terms of wisdom, so will improve the response to the parenting challenges. The choice in a situation is personal. While am writing all this, our journey as parents is not at all easy for us. It has always brought the biggest of the turmoil within ourselves. We have felt broken from within as we have faced immense negativity and anger, time and again. So many of our efforts have gone down the drain. Yet, this is our test and we need to pass by at least not going down level when faced with very difficult parenting situations.

- It is not about sending to the best schools, and giving the best food, clothing, and toys, that way, the rich parents would be the best parents to give everything that the child asks for. It's only about providing the right settings, the right atmosphere for the child to be whoever he/she wants to be (authentic experience)–Resilience and ability to respond.

Vedic teachings on birth and parenting (Garbhopanishad)

One of the fundamental beliefs that I go by is that existence is not limited to my knowledge or awareness or what I perceive using my five senses. It is much above and beyond. Just because something is not part of my experience, or I haven't been able to fully experience it in my life, doesn't mean it may not exist.

The fact that I am open to learning is because I acknowledge that there is and will always be more than I know or would know at any point in time.

For the same reason, I strongly feel that the creation is not a random phenomenon, it is an intelligent design. The science we know today may not have all the answers, but someday either our knowledge of science will evolve to answer many of our questions and provide substantial proof or we will evolve enough to have experiences beyond the five senses.

Till then let's hear it from the Vedas which talk about human construct.

As per Vedas the thinking, feeling, and choosing action cycle in our life is behind all manifestations or creations. Each individual is unique because of the way he/she thinks, feels, and acts.

This thinking, feeling, and acting cycle forms the specific energy pattern or template in a human being. It plays the biggest role even in conception and life afterward.

Sri Vidya explains the conception of a human being as the interaction between three energy patterns–Father, mother, and the cosmic complex that is to be born.

When men and women come together with an intention, their energy templates (thinking, feeling, acting nature) are superimposed. If that superimposed energy template matches with the energy template of any cosmic complex, the manifestation of a new universe in the form of a human being takes place.

This energy transaction is mirrored in the world of physical reality with the fusion of male and female to form a zygote.

Male–Giver of life energy and receiver of spiritual energy

Female–Receiver of life energy and giver of spiritual energy

Every human being is a universe in itself. We can say a human being is a single unit of the whole universe just like the way the cell is the unit in our body universe. And every human being is made of

1. Three Gunas or nature- Sattvik, Rajsik or Tamsik
2. Five Tatvas or elements- Air, Water, Fire, Space and Earth
3. Seven Chakras or Lokas or talas depending on the desires born out of thinking, feeling, choosing -Mooldhara chakra/ Root chakra (survival), Swadhistana chakra/Sakral chakra (pleasures), Manipura chakra/Solar plexus chakra (Status), Anahata/heart chakra (Social acceptance), Vishuddhi/throat chakra (Philosophy, charity, social work), Ajna/ the third eye chakra (external knowledge-intuition, perception), Sahasrara chakra / Crown chakra (wisdom
4. Nine Grahas or type of intelligence–Sun gives rhythmic intelligence, Moon gives emotional intelligence, Mars gives kinaesthetic intelligence, Mercury gives Verbal intelligence, Jupiter gives Spiritual Intelligence, Venus gives Scientific Intelligence, Saturn gives moral intelligence, Uranus gives Interpersonal intelligence and Neptune gives Intrapersonal intelligence)

It's a journey from a mere survival-based animal-like nature to becoming godly in terms of pure and unconditional love and highest wisdom. That's why they say the energy needs to move up from root chakra (survival) to crown chakra (pure wisdom) There are various ways to achieve that as described by the scriptures while we experience a human life. One of the ways to reach a higher level is by transcending our challenges. And that is why giving birth is a divine opportunity to learn and evolve for parents as it throws different challenges to different people. It is not an act of merely rearing and breeding.

Parenting is supposed to push us to limits - Whatever weakness we need to work on, whatever energy pattern we need to correct, our children are born to make sure that all such weaknesses get completely exposed and we are pushed to the limits. Whatever we didn't like in ourselves, our children will project the same. If you believe yelling is bad, you will find every reason to yell to become aware of what exists within you. The real test is not when the situation is in favour. Tests only happen when everything around us is not in our favour. It is not logical the way we think it should be; it is not what we like.

Unconditional love and acceptance are supposed to be the result out of all parenting challenges. Whenever it gets challenging, it is supposed to be that way, as there is a specific lesson behind all the pain that we go through.

What is it that we can do? What is our part as parents?

From intention to conception to introducing the world to passing on knowledge, beliefs, values & behaviours, parents have a huge role to play. And it can't be an act of blindness.

As per Vedas 3 months before the conception till 2 years of infancy is the golden period of education (time to create the right settings or sow the seed of human values by creating the impressions into the subconscious) for the new life. This is when a huge difference can be made in terms of epigenetics, metaphysical and educational knowledge transfers.

Golden period

Pre-conceptions- 3 months -100 days

Pregnancy–9 months- 280 days

Infancy–2 years–730 days

Total -1100 days of golden period

This is when parents work with their energy in specific energy fields created at every phase.

Benefits of Golden period education for the child

- Foundation for best life experiences
- Helps in establishing higher learning for later education
- Fulfilling the purpose of creation
- Helps in being grounded in knowledge & balanced in life

So, let's discuss our role in each phase

Wanting to-be-parents

1. Plan to conceive only when you are mentally and physically ready. Be really sure. It's not important to become a father or a mother just to feel whole. It's not important to become a parent just because your parents are saying so or your society is demanding so. It's not important to become a parent to add to some change or newness in life or to add to entertainment of a different kind. It's not important to become a parent because you want a Sachin Tendulkar in your house or because you want to dress your daughter like a princess just the way you imagined. More important is to provide the right environment for the life you intend to bring to this world. If you can't give a good, loving environment to a child, you will not only a create an unhappy individual but add to this unhappy, chaotic world. Just because it a natural process doesn't mean it needs to be a mindless act. Do not become a parent unless you truly want to be a parent and unless you have found the partner who will support your parenting journey. Giving birth & upbringing a life is a spiritual process and we are responsible for the kind of children we leave behind.
2. Once you have decided to be a parent, the first thing is to **set the right intention to bring up a life. The intention with which a human being is conceived defines the entire life experience.**

Pray, pray pray for a good soul to come into your lives. Pray for a healthy child. Most importantly, set an intention to be the best version of yourselves as parents. I should become the right parent, the most loving parent for my child. That's it. Boy or girl, Sachin Tendulkar or Lata Mangeshkar, 99% marks or a footballer, we must leave every expectation behind. Remember to focus on only your duty and your part. It is because of expectations that the essence of parenting gets lost. Dowry is an expectation; my child will take care of my finances in old age is an expectation. My child will have name, fame, and wealth is an expectation. All of this is mostly a personal agenda, not a selfless, unconditional love.

3. Secondly, **start your inner work that is working on self when it comes to anxiety, fear, anger or any other issues that you may have**. Learn parenting as it is not natural the way we have thought all along, it needs to be cultivated.
4. Couples should discuss their parenting beliefs and align themselves before planning. Discussing parenting beliefs and aligning on key aspects before planning to have children is indeed a crucial and wise approach. This proactive communication helps to build a strong foundation for co-parenting and can contribute to a healthier and more harmonious family environment.
5. Read and learn. Parents who learn and evolve in their lives conceive children with higher spiritual energies. Meaning, if the energy pattern of the parents' gets better, the life that comes to you will be of a higher quality in terms of energy pattern. Good energy pattern means good destiny because the choices made will be in the right direction. Surround yourself with inspiring & positive things, be it books or company or anything that you watch or listen to.

To-be-Parents

Not much time lost. At this stage too a lot can be done to ensure the well- being of the child. Apart from all the above step that need to be continued, it is good to start listening to Garbh Sanskar mantras and message to facilitate the whole process. Isha yoga, Coimbatore also runs a pregnancy course for to be parents just in case you would like to explore. There would be many other places too where one can do spiritual courses relevant for to-be-parents.

Now let's understand what happens in the 9 months period as per Vedic scriptures and why it is important to learn. This is the time when physical development of the foetus is fuelled by the unfolding of the kundalini life energy. Coiled kundalini is the spiritual heart. And the spiritual heart is the very seat of knowledge and existence. Connection between the microcosm and macrocosm knowledge of human construct is invoked in the spiritual heart of the cosmic being. Spiritual heart intelligence is activated much before the physical heart is formed.

As the pregnancy progresses, the coiled kundalini unfolds as chakras during pregnancy & continues till infancy and up to teenage.

How the unfolding of Kundalini life energy takes place

Conception is when parents' (thinking, feeling, choosing) energy patterns are superimposed to form a new energy pattern. The centre of any energy pattern is the reason or desire due to which we create life experiences. The thinking, feeling and choosing cycle spins due to the reason or desires to move ahead or for the life to continue. Understanding this cycle can provide insights into human behaviour and decision-making processes. It reflects the dynamic interplay between cognition, emotions, and the motivations that guide individuals through their life journey.

From where does the reason or desire come? It is provided by intellect.

As per Garuda purana, Grahas or planets take on the role of the intellect providers to human life. Grahas are cosmic beings or spinning energies that result from the crystallization of the collective human intellect and govern the laws of womb experience. The vibrations of the human realm are patterned by Grahas.

It is important to know that each month of pregnancy is governed by a specific type of intelligence.

Month 1 Scientific or mathematical intelligence. Graha or planet of influence–Shukra (Venus)

Influences on life - Behaviour, Attitude, Beauty, Passion

Risk of disorders - Malformation, OCD, Diabetes, Kidney, addictions, reproduction issues

Month 2 Kinaesthetic intelligence. Graha or planet of influence–Mangal (Mars)

Influences on life - Physical energy, Stamina

Risk of disorders - anger, aggression, extremes

Month 3 Scientific or mathematical intelligence. Graha or planet of influence–Guru (Jupiter)

Influences on life - Logical reasoning, Philosophy, Balance, Consistency, measured approach

Risk of disorders - Obesity

Month 4 Rhythmic intelligence. Graha or planet of influence–Surya (Sun)

Influences on life - Leadership, exploration, wanderlust, parental instincts

Risk of disorders - heart issues, loneliness

Month 5 Emotional intelligence. Graha or planet of influence–Chandra (Moon)

Influences on life - Behaviour, Attitude, Beauty, Passion

Risk of disorders - Over sensitive, Indigestion, Milk allergy, lack of concentration

Month 6 Moral intelligence. Graha or planet of influence–Shani (Saturn)

Influences on life - Order, Sequence, Structure, Consistency

Risk of disorders - Indiscipline, distorted organs, laziness, unconcerned.

Month 7 Verbal intelligence. Graha or planet of influence–Mercury (Budha)

Nervous system is developed around this time.

Influences on life - Intelligence, Speech, Fine arts

Risk of disorders - Skin problem, Addictions, Inconsistency, Nervousness

Month 8 Peak of progression/depression. Graha or planet of influence–Lord of Aadhana Lagna. The Umbilical cord is formed, and it supplies food to the child.

Influences on life - Body alignment, perception, mood, practicality

Risk of disorders - Spiritless witted, Perversion

Month9 - Preparing for birth. Self-motivation Graha or planet of influence–Chandra (Moon). Baby feels thirst and hunger.

Influences on life - Organising, arrangement, perseverance, moving on

Risk of disorders - Restlessness, Indecisive, mental psychic issues, Coordination issues.

Month 10 Birth, Graha or planet of influence–Surya (Sun)

Planets Rahu (Uranus) and Ketu (Neptune) also enter after the child is born.

While I have shared the above based on Vedas, it is not necessary to make this religious. Prayer can be done in any language as per what your religion says. Even a pure intention that comes from the heart of parents is enough. Just by knowing what is happening in each month, you can ensure that your intentions and actions and prayers are affecting certain intelligence in the child, so take care and ensure to do your part well. Child developing a positive quality or a negative quality is dependent on the education imparted by parents by their own conduct during the pregnancy. Children are influenced by a combination of genetic predispositions and the environments in which they grow and learn. While parental conduct during pregnancy and early childhood is important, it is just one piece of the puzzle in understanding and supporting a child's development.

Remember, prenatal education facilitates the learning of a child in the womb itself. Prenatal education involves management of influencing forces (including Grahas/planets) and defining higher purpose and meaning for life.

Parents

We as parents introduce the world to our child. We need to make sure that we give the right introduction.

Parents of a newly born child do have 2 more years of the golden period left to impart the knowledge to the child. Besides, till the time the child is 8 years, whatever the child hears, sees and experiences becomes part of his permanent memory. Hence it is extremely important on the parents' part, teachers' part and on part of everyone and anyone else around the child to ensure that the impression created in the child's mind are only positive and supportive of his/her growth.

Why tell the child

- Weather is changing, you will catch a cold. Wear a sweater or else you will fall sick.
- Don't fall or don't run, you will fall.
- Do this or listen to me or else a ghost will come.
- God punishes.
- We can't afford to have this or that.
- Life is difficult, earning is not easy.
- Look at him. He is a good boy; he comes first in the class.

Why not say the following instead or put the following beliefs in your child using words, actions and your own energy?

- Wear a sweater, be careful when weather changes.
- Be careful while running.
- Listening is good.
- God is loving and cares for everyone.
- We will buy it one day.
- Life is beautiful. It's easy to earn money, you only need to learn how.
- The body knows to heal itself. You have an excellent immune system.
- You are a precious child, unique. No one is like you, no one can ever be like you.

- There is abundance everywhere. The sky, the trees, mother earth, ocean.
- You are supported by the universe. Life supports you. You are loved… so on and so forth.

It's a well-known fact that our brain catches only the positive words. If you say don't fall. Brain picks up the word 'fall' first. Hence, sentences need to be modified in such a way that what you want the child to do becomes clearer and obvious without negative warnings as far as possible.

Then avoid instilling any fear or anxieties that you may have. Imagine how it would be to live freely without someone telling you the set definitions of good boy and good girls all the time based on what the majority of the society believes in.

Why should children have any fear of making mistakes? Don't we all do mistakes? Unless we allow that how will the seed of entrepreneurship be sown in our kids? Or how will the child know how to explore and enhance themselves?

Risk taking is inversely proportional to the fear of failure and making mistakes. And risk-taking ability is important anytime people want to do things differently from entrepreneurship to sports to inventions to art.

It's ok for kids also to make mistakes, when we allow ourselves and other elders to make mistakes. From our spouses to bosses to mother in laws to politicians, who doesn't go wrong. Why do kids have to be so perfect… not throw things, not spill things, follow what is being told exactly as it is? Is it fair just because they are small?

The other day I was in a metro where a young mother was hitting the child who was less than 2 years old because the child wasn't sitting in one place and was trying to walk in the train. Does the child of this age even understand what a train means and that balancing is difficult?

I have seen so many examples of this expected perfection among kids from parents… a kid whose brain is not yet fully developed and is just learning about the world is expected to be apt in his behaviours and actions as compared to fully grown adults. What a shame!

Yes, the kids have to be guided; they have to be informed about the consequences of their choices, but all this should come with a lot of love, a lot of freedom for them so that they can try & experiment in a positive environment with broad structure. The right environment is definitely our responsibility for sure.

If we all had a personal God, how would we want that god to be?

Unconditionally loving, someone with open arms to accept us exactly as we are, someone who would listen and care and contain all our emotions, including all outbursts, without hitting back. Someone we would go to, to heal ourselves and our lives. Right?

I feel that's what a parent should really mean to a child in this world - a personal, easily accessible God.

Now let's talk about step-by-step process to impart education and value system to the child, which is part of setting the right environment so that we can reduce some of the challenges in this role. While these are from Vedas, these are very much aligned to the science of human life as per ages.

As per the Vedas there are 16 milestones of education and empowerment (Sanskar) for the child where parents and grandparents and family have to play their role. And out of these 16 milestones, 3 are done during pregnancy, when the child is in the womb... (*Saskar se Sanskari*)

1. 1st month (Garbhadana)–Setting up the intention. Spiritual conception, as explained earlier. Here it is about working with our energy of intention in the universal energy field.
2. 3rd month (Pumsavana)–Gender identity is the milestone here. It is through prayers that we work with cosmic energy for a healthy child, irrespective of boy or girl. From here onwards, parents must start listening to Garb Sanskar mantras and music or anything that your respective religion suggests for the well-being of the child.
3. 7th month (Seemantonarayan)–Human cognition is the milestone here. We introduce the world, family and extended family to the to be born in the womb. Here again we work with in the universal energy field.

   After the birth of the child, there are six milestones of education that need to be completed within the infancy or 2 years. These are shishusanskars

4. At birth (Jaatkarma)–Health and immunity are the milestone here. This is the removal of waste from the body of the baby just after birth, which usually happens naturally. Symbolically ghee and honey is given to the child. It can be in almost negligible quantities as doctors suggest only mother's milk for at least 6 months. Doing things with prayers and awareness is something parents can do for the wellbeing of the child.
5. Early weeks (Nishkramana)–Milestone is establishing contact with the nature. Education is sensory. This is when parents introduce the child to elements of nature, elders, and deities.

Child is taken out of the house for the first time, by parents to go to a temple.

6. Naming ceremony (Naamkarana)–Milestone is naming the child or personality. Education is about identity during early weeks and months. Done by parents and family.
7. Introduction to food (Annaprashan)–Milestone is the intake of human food. Education is sensory. This is primarily to wean away the child from the mother at a proper time. Second, it warns the mother to stop breastfeeding the child at the right time.
8. Introduction to direction and spaces around (Karnaveda)–Milestone here is balance and movement. The education is spatial and directional. Parents, family and the society are involved here.
9. Chudakram–Milestone here is a completion of brain structure. Education is sensorial. Parents, family and the society are involved here.

Between the age of 2 yrs to 12 years

10. Vidyarambha–To foster the growth of the mind and cultivate intellectual prowess in the child, the Vidhyarambha sanskar is conducted typically when a child begins their early education, usually between the ages of 4 to 6 years old. This sacred ritual marks the rightful commencement of knowledge acquisition. While formal schooling may impart academic knowledge and pave the way for material success, true wisdom stems from nurturing the emotional core, aligning thoughts with righteousness, and embracing the divine purpose of life

11. Upanayansamskaraisalsofamousforitsnameas YAGNOPAVIT (janoi) SAMSKAAR. 'Upa' means near and 'nayana' means'to take to' hence taking the child to a teacher. This samskaar is very important to develop the child intellectually as well as mentally also practical and spiritual progress is recognized. The child, at this stage, enters studentship and disciplinary life
12. Praishyartha or Vedarambha–This is the ceremony of beginning of learning the Vedas, Upanishads and other scriptures. For other religions too, this is the time to start teaching what the respective holy scriptures are all about.

Above 12 years of age

13. Ritushuddhi/Keshanta–First shave for boys and for girls the it's about the first time their menstrual cycle starts. As parents, it is time to educate them about the hormonal changes that our bodies go through and how to deal with them. We as parents must educate our children about our bodies, hormonal changes and sexuality so that the information doesn't come to them from wrong sources.
14. Samaavaitana–Completion of formal education basically graduation ceremony that we all celebrate. This is the time, we prepare our children for the world out there.
15. Vivah Sanskar–Marriage ceremony. It involves families and friends included extended relations. This marks the beginning of a new life for anyone. Education is important at this stage as well both to the boy and to the girl. The importance of love and respect for each other, how to adjust, how to fulfil duties towards each other all should be ideally explained to the couple

16. Anthyeshthi–The last rites performed for any human as per their respective religions.

    Apart from these milestones of education on human life from birth to death, there is one important lesson for the modern times which every parent must educate his/ her child on and that is, 'how to handle failures'?

Let me tell you a story

Once upon a time, there lived a brilliant young man who excelled in science, achieving top scores in school and later securing admission to IIT. His academic success continued as he pursued an MBA at the University of California and landed a high-paying job in the USA.

He married a lovely Tamil woman, bought a spacious five-bedroom house, and owned several luxury cars. On the surface, his life seemed perfect, a hunky-dory tale of modern success. However, tragedy struck years later when the same man took his own life after killing his wife and children.

The California Institute of Psychology conducted a study to understand what led to this devastating outcome. They discovered that the man had lost his job during an economic downturn in America and struggled to find employment despite lowering his salary expectations.

Unable to keep up with mortgage payments, he eventually lost his home. Financial hardships pushed him to the brink, resulting in the unthinkable.

It was concluded, that the man was programmed for success but wasn't trained to handle failures.

I have already spoken multiple times about building resilience and the importance of how we respond to events. As parents, it's crucial that we instill in our children the belief that the best habit for success is learning to handle failures. We must teach them not to collapse when they lapse, starting by setting an example in dealing with failures and disappointments in life."

Part 7

Health & Well-being– As No 1 priority

Health &Well-being should be the priority even before happiness. Because happiness (Good feeling inside) is a chemical event in our brain and that itself depends on our physical and mental well-being or health. Physical and mental health is the result of the choices we make, so when we choose our health, we automatically choose our happiness too.

Whichever role we need to play whether it is of a parent or a spouse or an employee or a friend, we can only do it well when our body and mind supports us and when we make choices that support our mind and body health and well-being.

Going back to what we have learnt earlier, we need to work on all inputs to have health-food, water, air and thoughts. Any doctor who just treats the symptom and not a person as a whole is not doing a complete job. Any medical education which only talks about treating the symptom is incomplete and this applies especially in chronic cases, lifestyle diseases.

And finally, everything boils down to our choices that we make every moment. So can we say, to treat anyone, the first thing is to correct the choices at all levels, from eating to thinking?

Choosing happiness means making the right choices for good health & well-being at all levels. Choosing happiness is an ongoing process of making conscious decisions that prioritize your well-being across various dimensions of life. It's about recognizing the interconnectedness of physical, mental, and emotional health and actively making choices that contribute to a more fulfilling and joyful life. Our daily routine is a good indicator of our choosing to be happy. Our lifestyle is a good indicator of our choosing happiness over pain.

Isn't it obvious that a person choosing happiness would value his body, his mind, and his life above any short-term attractions or distractions? A person choosing to be happy would care and value himself/herself enough to be ready to make even hard choices in the present for his/her long term good.

Choices with only short term feel good in mind is greed

Choices with long term good in mind lead to happiness

Good health does need good judgement of the long- term consequences about the present actions & choices on part of the person who wants to be healthy & happy.

The way parenting has to be learnt, being healthy too, has to be learnt and practiced. Just because what we see for years in our homes and in our society around, it may not be the best thing to do or the ultimate solution.

"My father took alcohol every day and nothing happened to him so I can too". "I have seen my father smoking, and he never got cancer whereas Mr. Sharma, who is so disciplined, doesn't even have non-veg got cancer".

To all these statements, I have only one answer.

We all are unique and there are too many variables affecting us. Besides, the gap between our choices and results is not immediate every time, making it all the more difficult to understand why and how part of things.

There is so much that we don't know. Why something happens to one person and not the other?

The only thing we can do right is our part. Let's become selfish when it comes to choosing what to learn from others, as we can only afford to copy things that support our body and mind.

No need to blindly follow things just because they are feel good in the short term. Please explore yourself. Study and experiment yourself from food to nutrition to mental health. Read labels, manufacturing dates and list of ingredients before buying any product. Be aware. Then see what works for you and makes you feel healthy and energetic.

Every generation is supposed to be smarter than the previous one, then why not become more mindful and conscious of health too?

Why are we becoming dependent on medicines and not working on our choices first? Is it just because gulping medicine is easier than working on ourselves? I am not against or for any medical system.

There is enough medical research on how food impacts health, on how our thinking impacts health, then why doctors only prescribe medicines.

Why we haven't yet arrived at a system in which when someone suffers from any long-term issue, there is a team of doctors to help with every aspect of well-being. Why are we taking short cuts in medical fields which is simply telling our body to stop complaining using medicines from allopathy, homeopathy or ayurveda considering the way all systems are being practiced generally at present?

Some naturopathy institutes and alternative systems do try to help people with correcting their choices during their short-term courses, but they are not sustainable since the moment person is out of those programs, there is any easy solution, a pill that sells for a few rupees.

The amount of belief we have on pills is nowhere near the belief that we have on ourselves. Who wants to make hard choices, the choice of discipline when it's easy to take the pill and continue old ways unless the system breaks down completely someday and one starts questioning his/her own belief systems?

Food itself is a medicine, sunshine is a necessity. How we think or process our emotions do make a huge difference to our health. Why not first work on the basics?

There are always things beyond our control. Let's at least have the intention and action part right. Most importantly, only going to the gym will not help unless food and thoughts also are addressed along. Only doing yoga will not help if one is not taking enough nutrients or is not going out in the sun.

Mind+ body. Mind + Body. Mind + Body

Emphasising the fact that both are equally important and have to be addressed together to solve anything.

Things that make a huge difference to our health and well being

- Walking in the sun every day. And for some time being barefoot just to be in touch with the ground.
- Physical exercise and meditation every day to detox body and mind.
- Paying attention to what we eat, how we eat and when we eat before how much to eat.
- Keeping our body system alkaline (Ref to previous chapters). Avoid starting the day with tea or coffee or milk.
- Fasting at least once in 15 days and giving a water enema to clean intestines once in 15 days during a fast day.
- Getting up early and giving at least 3 hrs gap between dinner and sleep time. One of the most important things.

While our body is an intelligent design, we do have an excretory system to throw the waste from our bodies and sleep to do the same from our mind as did our ancestors. However, the times we are living in are not the same due to continuous body and mind evolution due to the changing environments. In both the areas, our challenges have increased due to the abundance of options and increase in consumption.

We eat much more than our early ancestors did; and we eat a greater number of times. We don't work as physically hard as they did.

At mind level, we have a huge amount of exposure today. Too many things are happening around in the society and in the world thanks to media and information flow. We form too many impressions and jump to conclusions on an everyday basis. So, for both mind and body, our cleaning mechanism too has to evolve further and become more robust.

Just like our cleaning mechanisms for the physical environment, it's equally important to prioritize the development and enhancement of mechanisms for mental and emotional well-being. That's why additional steps like meditation and fasting or water enema is being practiced in present times.

For additional reading, have included food chart in this book to help you understand which type of food contains what. Please refer to the same for more information.

Part 8

Importance of Sleep

Have you heard about Randy Gardner's sleep deprivation experiment done in 1964?

Randy Gardner was a 17 yrs old high school student who had volunteered for the sleep deprivation experiment which lasted for a total of 264 hrs which is approx. 11 days. This was done in Randy Gardner's home in California. Throughout the experiment, Gardner was closely monitored by two researchers: Robert C. Gunn and William C. Dement.

The following were the findings:

In the first few days of the experiment, Gardner remained relatively alert and active by engaging in activities like playing basketball and ping-pong.

Hallucinations: Around the third day without sleep, Gardner began experiencing hallucinations. He reported seeing objects that weren't present and hearing sounds that weren't there.

Cognitive Decline: As the days progressed, Gardner's cognitive function declined significantly. He had difficulty concentrating, remembering basic information, and solving simple problems.

Mood Changes: Gardner's mood became increasingly unstable. He swung between moments of euphoria and irritability, displaying emotional volatility.

Delusional Thinking: Gardner exhibited delusional thinking, such as claiming to have broken a record for sleep deprivation (though there was no official record at the time). This indicated impaired judgment.

Physical Symptoms: Gardner experienced physical discomfort, including blurred vision, slurred speech, and muscle aches.

Recovery: After the experiment concluded, Gardner slept for 14 hours straight. He reported feeling groggy upon waking.

Thankfully this was done in a controlled environment under supervision otherwise the results could have been far worse.

No surprise the Chernobyl Disaster in 1986, Exxon Valdez Oil Spill in 1989 as well as three mile island nuclear accident in 1979, all happened due to sleep deprived operators. Yet, how many of us give importance to our sleep when it's a party, when its late night movie or work which only starts after 9 pm.

Have you observed an infant who has not slept well? They become so cranky. Just borne are simple. When they are hungry, they cry. When they are sleepy, they cry. When they need love and warmth, they cry. However, as we grow, we tend to start taking things for granted especially our sleep.

When the mind needs rest, we spend time looking at reels on the phone or do binge watching. Social media to soap opera, everything is made with the intent that we stick to it and find it difficult to leave even when it's an absolute requirement by our body. The irony is the discomforts of the mind show up at a later stage. And most cases, even the body health issues may not be easily relatable.

Input and output both are important when it comes to our body and mind. Imagine what would happen if we keep eating but are not able to take the waste out. Physical discomforts are more obvious in life for us to take clue from and change our course of actions but what about mental cleansing? Sleep is the nature's way of cleaning our mind and restoring our systems. One may not meditate on a regular basis but sleeping well every night is a basic necessity of a human life.

There is no fixed formula for number of hours. Individual sleep needs can vary, and factors such as age, genetics, lifestyle, and overall health can influence how many hours of sleep one needs.

Setting up a proper body clock would help mind and body to understand how to respond accordingly. It's like once you set a pattern or program in your mind the mind learns to rerun the same program and body does its functions basis that.

Prioritizing sleep by establishing a regular sleep schedule, creating a comfortable sleep environment, and practicing good sleep hygiene hence is an intelligent way of living and supporting our own well-being.

Here's are a few tips for a good night's sleep

- Most importantly, the direction to put your head shouldn't be north at all if you are in the northern hemisphere to avoid the magnetic pull. Normally in a wakeful state, our blood flow is impacted by gravitational pull. We are designed in such a way the heart limits the amount of blood it pumps to the head. If it is more than what's needed by our system, it would obviously be dangerous. In a sleep state, blood flow is already against gravity. Since our blood has iron, there are chances of blood flow getting impacted by the magnetic pull of north which would mean not only disturbed sleep but also negative health impact (physiological problems over a period of time) . The best direction is usually east to put your head or else south if you must in northern hemisphere.
- Sleep at least 3-4 later than your dinner. Good sleep requires light stomach.
- Taking a shower before going to bed does make a lot of difference. It's a kind of purification and does work well. Luke warm water is good enough.
- Chant or pray just before sleeping

- Switch off all the electronic gadgets at least two hours before bedtime. Engage in reading to naturally tire your eyes, preparing for better sleep.

Let's see what a good sleep does to us-

1. **Healing and Restoration:** One of the scariest things for my 76 year old mother is not being able to sleep well. It's true. Her sugar level, BP level all change and she develops confusion. Sleep is a time when our body undergoes essential restorative processes. It helps in repairing and healing our cells, tissues, muscles and allows our body and systems within to recover from the wear and tear of our everyday lives. Sleep plays a crucial role in the formation of immune memory, which is essential for mounting effective immune responses against pathogens encountered previously. Quality sleep strengthens the immune system's ability to recognize and combat infections, improving overall immunity.
2. **Emotional Well- being:** Sleep is very important for our emotional well being because emotions directly impact the body health too. Good sleep regulates our emotions. Adequate sleep can enhance emotional stability and coping mechanisms, reducing the risk of mood disorders like depression and anxiety. Lack of sleep can lead to mood swings, irritation, anxiety and even depression while a good sleep can automatically bring emotional resilience and stability. So, now you know. To have resilience while facing your toughest life situations, do sleep well.
3. **Cognitive function:** Want good memory, then sleep well. Want good grasping power, learning and problem solving ability then sleep well. If you want to be creative, then sleep well. Sleep

brings clarity and that's what we need in life to make right choices and decisions. During sleep, the brain consolidates information and experiences, facilitating novel connections and insights that may not be apparent during wakefulness.

4. **Physical health:** Adequate sleep is associated with a reduced risk of various health issues, including cardiovascular diseases, diabetes, obesity, and immune system dysfunction. A good sleep also aids healthy metabolism.

5. **Immune system:** During sleep, our immune system works to fight off infections and illnesses. What happens in viral fever? We become less active. We hardly eat. But we sleep a lot. All of this happens naturally due to body's intelligent system.

   For our immune system to do its job well, all our energies have to support it which can only happen when energies are not being used up for other purposes like digestion or exercising or mental work. Sleep allows cells to repair DNA damage, replenish energy stores, and regulate cellular functions, contributing to overall tissue health and longevity. On the other hand imagine consistent sleep deprivation can weaken our immune system's ability to respond effectively to threats.

6. **Hormone regulation:** Sleep plays a significant role in regulating hormones, including those that control appetite, stress response, growth, and reproductive functions. Adequate sleep helps maintain optimal hormone levels, supporting overall health and well-being. Disruption in sleep patterns can lead to hormonal imbalances.

7. **Cell Repair:** This is especially for children, adolescents and athletes. Who doesn't want good height, strong muscles and bones? Do you know your sleep helps in release of growth

hormones that aid in repairing and building tissues, muscles, and bones? During deep sleep stages, the body releases growth hormone, which promotes muscle repair and regeneration. Going to gym is not enough, eating protein is not enough. Sleeping on time is also necessary to become big and strong.

8. **Brain Detoxification:** Recent research suggests that the brain's glymphatic system becomes more active during sleep, helping to remove waste products and toxins that accumulate during wakefulness. This process helps maintain brain health and may reduce the risk of neurodegenerative diseases like Alzheimer's.
9. **Performance:** Getting adequate sleep enhances our energy levels and overall physical performance. It's crucial for athletes, professionals, and anyone who needs to stay alert and productive throughout the day. And who doesn't want to be productive in this competitive world.
10. **Safety:** Thankfully pilots are not allowed to fly the plane without rest. Sleep deprivation impairs motor skills, reaction times, and decision-making, which can lead to accidents and injuries. Operating vehicles or heavy machinery without proper sleep can be dangerous.

Hence, very basic tool to get better at facing tough situation is to sleep well. For good things to come in, not so good has to go out. Our mind needs cleaning to start afresh every day.

Part 9

The Most Important and Powerful Lesson

Once, a disciple approached his guru with a fervent desire to meet Buddha. "What should I do?" he asked, revealing that he had been diligently meditating for a year. The guru, with serene wisdom, advised him to continue meditating for five more years before seeking the meeting. Trusting his guru's guidance, the disciple returned to his practice.

Years drifted by like whispers in the wind, yet the disciple's fervor remained unyielding. Despite, his unwavering dedication, the elusive encounter with Buddha seemed distant.

Disheartened, the disciple returned to his guru, seeking solace and understanding. He said to his Guru, 'I meditated for 5 years, did everything as you said but nothing happened. I haven't met Buddha yet'.

With gentle reassurance, the guru urged him to persist, promising that Buddha would eventually come to meet him. Encouraged by his guru's faith, the disciple immersed himself once more into his meditation, following every discipline with renewed determination. He meditates again for 5 years but nothing happens.

He goes back to his guru asking the same question. Guru gives no reason. He again asks him to go back and meditate for another 5 years. The disappointed disciple goes back to meditation. Years passed, seasons changed, the body & the appearance changed, but he remained steadfast in his pursuit.

Then, one fateful day, amidst the silence of his meditation, he was startled awake by an unexpected presence. Before him stood a dog, afflicted with illness and covered in fleas, its appearance repelling to the eyes.

But within the depths of his heart, the disciple felt an overwhelming surge of pure, unconditional love.

Moved by compassion, he began to tenderly cleanse the dog's wounded body with his own tongue, an act of selfless devotion born from the depths of his being. In that moment, the veil of illusion dissolved, revealing the radiant presence of Buddha before him. The dog turned into Buddha himself due to the unconditional love that filled the disciples being.

All along I have been speaking about body, breath and mind but when I wasn't able to connect all the dots in my own life puzzle, I realized the missing link and the main ingredient was Love. It's not about being loved or getting love, it's about being able to love even when we don't like something within us or outside of us.

While we use the word love easily, probably a few enlightened ones only understand it fully. Most of us fail to understand the meaning especially when it comes out as a lesson from our most painful experiences or situations.

As a matter of fact, I am also trying my best to accept and love despite my dislikes. However, I do believe that, love is the common lesson for all of us irrespective of our stories, families or religion. Love is greater and always the most powerful thing in this world.

Love is what motivates us. Love for anything or anyone helps us find purpose and meaning in our lives. And of course, while love is the most important lesson, balance is the absolute necessity.

Love >Hatred

Love >fear

Love> Revenge

Love>Killings

Love> Success/ Wealth

Love > Social Image/Name/Fame

Love> Religion

We realize hatred, pain, fear; injustice much more than anything yet love is more powerful. To be able to love unconditionally, one needs courage, one needs refinement, and one needs awareness. However, feelings like hatred, fear etc can come easily because of our minds and our weaknesses. Anyone can hate, anyone can kill, anyone can misbehave or misuse his power.

All it requires is something we don't like. Love on the other hand needs mental strength. It's a higher quality. It needs accepting as it is without conditions or manipulations. But Oh! It is not so easy to develop this unconditional love. Not sure how many lifetimes are needed for people like us.

That's why most of us find it difficult to even love ourselves given our own set of likes and dislikes which affect us emotionally.

Do we want our God to be a source of love or a source of hatred? Do we want God to have conditions to love us? No, right? Then we better start playing God in our own lives. Love ourselves unconditionally. In other words, accepting things as it is in the present but taking action for what is right and in the highest good of all.

Love and acceptance are two sides of the same coin.

Word of caution - Acceptance doesn't ever mean letting people behave as they wish to or becoming a doormat for someone out of love. One may have love in their heart but there are times when strict actions on the outside may be needed. Acceptance simply is not getting emotionally attached or impacted but moving on with action.

Human progress or success is directly proportional to the amount of love and acceptance that develops within. This is a perspective rooted in the belief that personal growth and societal advancement are closely tied to emotional and social well-being.

Love and acceptance are often associated with emotional intelligence, which involves understanding and managing one's own emotions as well as understanding and empathizing with the emotions of others. Both encourage positive interpersonal relationships, both on an individual and societal level.

A supportive and accepting environment encourages creativity and innovation. When individuals feel safe to express themselves without fear of judgment or rejection, they are more likely to think outside the box, take risks, and explore new ideas. Love and acceptance contribute to the creation of inclusive communities and societies where diversity is celebrated and everyone has equal opportunities to thrive. When individuals cultivate love and acceptance within themselves, they experience greater happiness, resilience, and peace of mind.

The journey is towards becoming a source of love (Moving from *Maanav to Madhav* as per scriptures) and moving towards higher qualities.

I truly believe if we all knew true love and acceptance, we would have learnt everything. We can transcend above our instincts only when love increases and fills everything in our lives.

Imagine a killer who kills blindly without mercy. No matter what punishment is given to him, it would be less. But if this person's heart one day can feel the same amount of love for everyone as you do feel for your loved ones today, what would happen? Self-realization would make him go through, what the punishment prescribed by others can't.

It is difficult to do any harm when the heart is filled with pure love. Love that starts within and touches everyone without discrimination or conditions.

I will take another example –one of the pain points in modern world - Traffic. Say, if you driving on the road in a swanky car and there are a number of people doing mistakes starting from auto-rickshaw driver to bike rider to people walking on the road. What happens? You don't like the chaos. You get frustrated. You shout, you get angry. Some people also become abusive. Of course, there are reasons. There is a need to reach on time. Most people on road are unruly and don't follow the rules.

But what if you could look at everyone's story then and there? What if you could understand the struggle on everyone's part even if you saw them doing the mistake? What if you could feel more love towards everyone who is less privileged.

Think of it... What is the biggest problem? It's primarily the way we look at things or derive the meaning (Our thoughts). World view changes with love.

Receiving love doesn't make us as special as being able to love without expecting anything back. Only when we don't expect returns, our love can expand and reach people we don't even know. Expectations and attachment usually come in the way of love.

I expect to be understood and not misunderstood. I expect to be heard. I expect to be loved and respected. I expect to be spoken to nicely. I expect. I am attached to what I want and what I don't want and therefore I remain stuck. Every lesson starts and ends here for me... and I say, 'if only I knew to love without attachment'.

Part 10

How to Face Our Toughest Situations in Life

This chapter is quite challenging, as there exists no universal solution tailored to each individual's circumstances. Just as each of us are distinct, so too are our narratives and the requisite actions needed in any given scenario.

Nonetheless, the reservoir of tales depicting humanity's resilience against adversity, triumphing over obstacles, and ascending in life remains abundant. Allow me to share a selection of such stories

Arunima Sinha, a national-level volleyball player in India, faced a life-changing incident when she was thrown off a moving train by robbers. Despite losing a leg in the incident, she became the first female amputee to climb Mount Everest, showcasing incredible resilience and determination.

Malvika Iyer, a bomb blast survivor in India, lost both her hands in a bomb explosion at the age of 13. Instead of succumbing to despair, she pursued education, earned a Ph.D., and became a disability rights activist, motivational speaker, and social worker.

Dashrath Manjhi of Bihar India, also known as the "Mountain Man," single-handedly carved a 360-foot-long, 30-foot-wide, and 25-foot-deep path through a mountain using only a hammer and chisel over 22 years. His dedication and hard work shortened the travel distance between his village Gehlaur and the nearest town, proving the extraordinary feats individuals can achieve.

Sunitha Krishnan is a rape survivor channelled her traumatic experience into activism. She co-founded Prajwala, an organization dedicated to rescuing and rehabilitating victims of sex trafficking and sexual violence in India. Sunitha's tireless efforts have helped thousands of survivors rebuild their lives and have raised awareness about the issue of human trafficking and sexual exploitation.

Indeed, beyond the borders of India too, there exist narratives across every domain, spanning international sports, art, media, science and many other fields.

Ronaldo fought poverty, heart problem, setbacks almost everything to become a success story. Ronaldo's illustrious career has seen him win numerous individual awards, including multiple FIFA Ballon d'Or titles, cementing his legacy as one of the greatest footballers of all time.

Oprah Winfrey faced a challenging childhood marked by poverty and abuse. She overcame these obstacles to become one of the most influential and successful media moguls. Today, she is not only a billionaire but also a philanthropist and an inspiration to many.

Before becoming a successful actor and wrestler, Dwayne Johnson faced financial struggles and a failed football career. He battled depression and was cut from the Canadian Football League, but he reinvented himself and is now one of the highest-paid actors in Hollywood.

The author of the immensely popular Harry Potter series, J.K. Rowling, faced adversity as a struggling single mother. She battled depression and financial difficulties while writing the first Harry Potter book. Her perseverance paid off, and she is now one of the most successful authors in the world.

Robert Downey Jr. struggled with substance abuse and legal issues for many years. Despite multiple setbacks, he managed to overcome addiction and revived his career with iconic roles like Tony Stark/Iron Man in the Marvel Cinematic Universe.

Beyond the stories of celebrated individuals who overcome adversity and achieve greatness, there exists another side of the coin where many struggle tirelessly but go unrecognized for their talents and efforts during their lifetimes. These unsung heroes embody the spirit of resilience and fortitude, their stories often untold but nevertheless are poignant reminders of human courage to fight tough situations.

One such case is Leonardo Da Vinci who was an illegitimate child without any formal education or a degree. Despite excelling in everything from science to sculpture to painting, he never had any success to his name until 46 when he painted the last supper. Yet, one of the most gifted and innovative man in history, he had to struggle to find jobs and never received the due recognition while he was alive.

Vincent van Gogh, the famed Dutch painter, struggled with mental illness and poverty throughout his life. Despite producing some of the most celebrated works of art in history, van Gogh received little recognition during his lifetime and only achieved widespread acclaim posthumously.

Srinivasa Ramanujan was an Indian mathematician whose groundbreaking contributions to mathematics went largely unrecognized during his lifetime. Despite lacking formal training, Ramanujan made significant discoveries in number theory and mathematical analysis. However, his work only gained widespread recognition after being brought to the attention of prominent mathematicians like G.H. Hardy much later in life.

Alan Turing was another brilliant mathematician and code breaker whose efforts played a significant role in deciphering German codes during World War II, contributing to Allied victory. Despite his invaluable contributions, Turing faced persecution for his homosexuality and was not widely recognized for his achievements during his lifetime.

Then there are cases like Rosalind Franklin, a chemist whose work was crucial to the discovery of the structure of DNA. Despite her pivotal contributions, Franklin's role was largely overlooked during her lifetime, with credit for the discovery primarily going to James Watson and Francis Crick.

Last but not the least, the story of Mr Subhas Chandra Bose, a prominent leader in India's struggle for independence from British rule deserves respect. Despite his significant contributions to the freedom movement, including founding the Indian National Army (INA) to fight against British forces, Bose's role was overshadowed by other leaders and till date we are not able to find truth about his sudden disappearance.

I would say, all of us are heroes in our own sphere of life. Point is 2 plus 2 is not always 4 in life. There are times it's very difficult to find logic. Logic in someone's behaviour, logic in what one receives in life, logic in what happens to one in life.

We don't know the complete picture so there are no answers to why only Mr. X gets cancer despite being a fitness freak, why only Y fails in exam despite teaching her own classmates who scored better, why only Z got cheated by her spouse despite being such a nice person. There are stories where hard work paid off, there are stories where it didn't. So on and so forth.

Honestly, logic to the event is not as important as our reaction to the event is yet we all keep analysing trying to prove our situations and expect others to empathise but in vain.

Whenever I have faced my challenges, I have spent hours trying to find logic and have hardly found anyone who could genuinely empathise or understand, not even my spouse. In fact, we all tend to have maximum expectations from our partners and children and that's where we get disappointed.

No one can truly understand someone else's pain point even if he/she stands with you. This is a true and many a times words can't even express the exact details of the event one goes through to others so how is it possible for others to imagine, assume and understand unless they themselves go through it.

I believe that's why the karma theory makes so much sense. We can never understand what we do or have done till we go through the same pain ourselves. So, there is no point of comparison or judgement when looking at each others' challenges. We all have our own battles to fight and nothing is small or big.

Now, let's get to the point. - How do we go through what we have to and come out in one piece? It's a fact that there can't be one fixed solution for all? Besides, no one has the right to interfere with someone's free will so the choice of the action always remains with the individual.

But yes, there is guidance in our scriptures, there is guidance in science and there is guidance that comes from the collective experience.

To deepen the understanding, I will break the so called difficult or challenging situation into parts to analyse in order to find some clarity.

Let me take an example: Imagine, you had an amazing day at college. The girl you were so fond of for last 3 years finally spoke to you and even said she likes you. You come back home still in the same romantic and happy mood. At dinner table you find your mother has made something you don't like at all. How would you react when you are internally filled with feelings of love? Probably you won't even mind eating all that.

Now imagine you had a very bad day at work. Your boss insulted you in front of everyone. Your work wasn't appreciated and you couldn't even get time to eat lunch. You come back home having lost your energy. At dinner table, you get what you don't like at all. How would you react?

Both are facing the same situation but the internal state is different and that will determine not just the impact of the not so favourite food in front of you but also the reaction towards it.

Secondly let's say we interchange the two people. The college guy for whom the girl's attention is the most important thing in the world has a bad day at work. Boss insults him and he couldn't eat lunch. Work anyway doesn't mean much to him. How would he react at the not so favourite food on dinner table?

Points to note

The degree of the challenge or toughness in any situation is inversely proportional to the energy we have within us.

On the reverse, if our energy levels are intact or higher, we are in a much better position to face situations, our reactions would be mild or we may even let go. High levels of motivation and energy can provide the drive and resilience needed to tackle difficult situations with confidence and determination.

Secondly, the degree of challenge is directly proportional to the amount of weakness we have in any specific area based on karma (Thoughts, beliefs, values and self-identity). For each one of us, our challenge is the biggest because that's where our personal weakness is. I won't get affected by something that's not important to me in my head. I would be much more impacted by things that's are important to me.

For e.g. 'if keeping a word' is an important value in my eyes but not in others, it will not hurt someone else when the opposite happens as much as it will hurt me.

So, for obvious reasons, we can work on two things –

- **Keeping our energy levels high throughout so that when there is any sad and bad impact, the dip in the energy is not as much.** High levels mean the energy in higher states – e.g. creative energy or loving energy. Since energy can neither be created nor destroyed, energy changes forms within us. Love is high energy state, hatred is low energy state. Helping others is a high energy state. Revenge is low energy state. Living on instincts is operating from lower energy state. Living consciously is a high energy state where one is mindful of every expression.

  We need high energy state to deal with challenges better. They say in good mood, it's easy to ignore imperfections.

- **Addressing our weaknesses for more balance** - Weakness could be the result of our thoughts, beliefs, exposure or personality itself. And **the more baggage we have the more imbalances we create in our environment either by doing things not required at all or by not doing things which are truly required.**

  Identifying and working on our weaknesses allows us to continuously improve ourselves. By addressing areas where we are less proficient or effective, we can develop new skills, expand our knowledge, and enhance our capabilities.

  Understanding what's behind our behaviour & reactions is a way to address our weakness. Self-awareness allows us to recognize patterns of behaviour that may be unproductive or harmful, as well as identify the underlying emotions, beliefs, or experiences driving those behaviours.

  What's our latent need which makes us behave in a certain way? So that we learn to give less importance to what doesn't serve us over a period of time with deliberate practice.

Example – If toxic workplace is a big challenge, what am I giving importance to is the question! Is it not getting appreciated, not being heard or importance to what others think or how they behave or how just they are to me? If what others think and say is important then there lies the weakness.

Family and social system teaches us to care about what others think. In balance it is fine. We should be careful and sensitive towards others but when the same thing "what others think' goes out of balance then we have the challenge. This is just one example. There are for sure many ways to address our weaknesses but all that starts with accepting the weakness in first place and then taking actions.

How to achieve the high energy state?

In previous chapters I have already spoken about how to keep our energy states high from taking care of diet, exercise, company, meditation and more. Additional things like learning Art and music puts us in higher energy state.

Travelling, specifically going on treks or spiritual retreats can put us in higher energy states. Helping others can put us in high energy states. Shifting focus to the things which are good for self and others puts us in higher energy states.

Talking to a mentor, guide or even a close friend who can inspire puts us in higher energy states. Any work like writing or playing sport which needs full attention puts us in higher state. **If there are 100 things which put us down in life, we only have to find the other 100 which can lift us up. To reiterate it a conscious, continuous effort and practice.**

Please note: When the going gets really tough, its ok to cry, its ok to feel the feelings, its ok to process the emotions first. Take the needed time and then slowly get up again, to start again, to fight again with our own demons.

How to address our weaknesses?

I want to share two instances here.

This happened a few days back while I was at a friend's place around 8 – 8.30 pm discussing a business idea. In the middle of an intensive discussion, I get a call from another friend from college, crying on phone. Her voice was very disturbed and she said, 'Again everything is ruined, why it happens with me.'

Since that wasn't the right place and time to talk to her, I told her "Please give me some time, I will call you ASAP, I am with people". While I continued discussing the idea for some time, I couldn't hold my horses from running in all directions from life threatening diseases to much worse things on the basis of the voice on call. Somehow, I finished the work discussion, came back home and closed the door of my room to be able to listen to her properly.

Till date, I am so grateful that it wasn't about any of those things that passed through my mind. It was a challenging work situation.

Another thing happened today. This is about a client of mine who works in USA and has come home (India) in December. He was supposed to fly to Bali yesterday with his spouse to celebrate his anniversary but couldn't. They had applied for work visa permit renewal just after coming to India but couldn't get passports back on time from US consulate despite every attempt. They had been checking the site every minute, going to the consulate, going to the collection centre, sitting there for hours but in vain.

Despite the approval and stamping, the consulate denied to hand over the passports directly to them since as per rules it would be sent to the collection centre first which means waste of 2 days and cancelling the trip.

That was quite a financial loss. On top of that the trip was booked in August this year… it carried so much hope and excitement. I was really feeling bad for them and that's when my cook sent a message that her sister has fallen from the fourth floor and she is in coma.

Do I say more? This was a lesson- **While it's okay to see ourselves as the centre of our universe; we are not the centre of the whole universe**.

Addressing our own weaknesses requires going within ourselves after all we are only fighting against our own minds. This is questing ourselves in a nutshell and reasoning with ourselves. While it's a long way home, here are some SOS steps that can be used.

1. Deep breathing to relax and bring a little balance into our system in the time of crisis. If we lapse, we can't collapse. Attention to the present moment, just like walking on tight rope is the key. I also use mantra in my mind when gripped with fear or anger.
2. Taking a step back from the situation, going out, taking a break. If possible, leave the place or people for few minutes or hours to think clearly. Changing the place, environment or surroundings even for a little while helps.
3. If leaving the place is not possible, taking time to act when it's really tough and decision making is difficult. Reactions in the heat of the moment usually end up in remorse.
4. Break it down into what's in control and what's not. Further divide what's in control into manageable tasks. Embrace flexibility and focus on the solution than on the problem
5. Surrounding oneself with positive talks, books and people. Luckily these days we have access to so many wonderful ideas

and inspiring people due to internet. Books, podcasts, videos. What we intend to search for, we get.

6. Taking help from mentors, guides, friends or even elderly or at times younger ones at home who could provide positive support. Friends who hand over the whiskey bottle to boost the morale may not be a great idea in the long term.
7. Also, there is no harm in talking to therapists or counsellors. Different challenges require different experts and specialists.
8. Own efforts and introspection holds the highest value here- Keep asking why to yourself. Why this anger? Or why this fear? Why this feeling of wrong or injustice? What do I believe? Where are things like - it should be like this or it should not be like this, coming from? It's an art to learn how to use the mind to defeat the mind.
9. Always long-term thinking - At times, when the tide is against, even bowing before the foolish for the time being can be an intelligent idea. For example- When dealing with teenage jerks at home, on so many occasions parents simply let go and make their kids feel that they have won.

While I have written all ideas here, honestly, going through the challenges is very difficult for me too. Napolean Hill wasn't rich when he wrote, 'Think grow and rich' but eventually he got rich. I too am hoping to get more clarity and purity of mind, better hold on my weaknesses as I am writing this book.

Yesterday only I had an emotional breakdown. While I do so many things to work on my thinking, on my physical and mental health yet there are times when the energy I have within falls short to stay unaffected. When I try to stop reactions, the anger and pain for some time, usually it comes out in some other way or in a much bigger way.

I end up having reactions I don't like. When I looked for answers, I saw it coming from a feeling of helplessness being unacceptable to me. I have the tendency to sort out, to solve; just not ready to accept that no matter what I do, something's won't change.

We all suffer from one thing- Not accepting what we don't like. Be it any problem in the world. Our system revolts in pain to accept things we don't like at all, things we don't find as fair, things we don't find as right in our heads, not getting what we want, getting what we don't want. We either spend time analysing what's wrong with us or what's wrong with others. What mistakes we did or what wrong others did. Likes, dislikes, morals, value systems, principles, everything exists in our belief system which we form based on exposure and experience.

So, the answer is acceptance. Problem is non acceptance. Not at all easy or else everyone would have attained nirvana by now. Yet, small and steady steps of practice we can take every day, every time.

The fact remains we can't change what has happened at any point in life. It's over and done. And it is also a fact that everything is bound to change, nothing remains constant. First fact requires acceptance and second requires patience to wait till the change for good happens while we keep taking our actions.

I remember after I was back from Vipassana, initially I was in a good space. 10 days of no disturbance, only meditation. Obviously, my energy levels were in higher states. But only after a few days without regular practice, I started losing the energy (usage of energy depends on the quality of thoughts) & my system went into an auto reaction mode.

I was wondering, why is keeping energy levels high doesn't come naturally to us in this world?

Given that the real currency we have in life is energy, for our best performance and to face the challenging situations, we all need to move our energy up from lower chakras to higher chakras and increase it continuously.

If not move up, at least it shouldn't go down to avoid the worst. However, every interaction with the environment, depending on its nature, leads to change in our energy levels.

Thoughts and beliefs in repetition mode become behaviours and repeated behaviours become habits. Our thoughts and beliefs shape our perceptions, attitudes, and interpretations of the world around us. They can be conscious or subconscious and are influenced by various factors such as past experiences, cultural upbringing, and personal values.

Losing energy has also become a habit in most of us, more like an involuntary habit. Getting affected by any sort of nonsense is a habit. When we repeatedly think or believe in certain ideas or concepts, they become ingrained in our minds. Whereas the opposite that is gaining energy is not a habit yet. We need conscious effort from meditation to yoga to healthy lifestyle to close proximity to nature for gaining energy. Gaining and maintaining energy often requires conscious effort and intention. While our bodies have natural rhythms and energy cycles, external factors like stress, lifestyle choices, and environmental conditions can affect our energy levels.

I see this whole thing very similar as wanting to leave smoking habit. Whatever is required to stop smoking, similar approach may also work to stop getting emotionally affected by the same happenings or certain events every time. Who knows? I have heard of reframing behaviour modality in NLP. Individuals can change their perspective and response to a given situation, leading to more positive outcomes and behaviours. By reframing behaviour modality, individuals can break free from limiting beliefs and behaviours and create new patterns of thinking and acting that support their goals and aspirations.

Hypnotherapy too has helped many people alter their behaviours by changing the beliefs. Hypnotherapy involves inducing a relaxed state of consciousness, often referred to as a trance or hypnotic state. It also helps to reinforce the new beliefs and behaviours at the subconscious level. As the individual begins to internalize the new beliefs and behaviours, they can integrate them into their daily life and apply them in various situations.

Looking forward to the day when we humans would be able to alter our behaviours, change our tendencies and personalities permanently with absolute ease in no time. Till then, we have to continue to work at all the levels with available tools and techniques to keep bringing the mind back to track.

Summary

Broadly, there are two things we need to work on – Moving energy up in our system from lower levels (lower chakras or living on instincts) to higher levels (higher chakras or living consciously) and working on our weaknesses to avoid over thinking and unnecessary reactions.

The following chapter details how to enhance every aspect of ourselves, ensuring not only personal empowerment but also establishing a fail-safe system to tackle life's diverse challenges effectively.

Part 11

Designing Life–
A Step by Step Approach

Let me start with a classic story of King Ashoka the Great here – the mighty ruler of the Maurya Dynasty from 268 to 232 BCE.

In the early years of his rule, Ashoka was a formidable leader, known for his involvement in brutal military campaigns marked by ambition, power and insatiable thirst for expanding the Maurya Empire. However, destiny had a profound lesson in store for him—one that would teach him the importance of balance in life.

The turning point came with the Kalinga War in 261 BCE, a conflict that Ashoka ultimately won. However, victory came at a high cost, and the aftermath of the war left the once-mighty king in a state of deep pain. The widespread devastation and the overwhelming loss of life on a massive scale haunted Ashoka, and the taste of triumph was bitter in the face of such human suffering.

In the aftermath of conquest, Ashoka discovered life balance through a transformation. Embracing non-violence and compassion, he prioritized spiritual and moral well-being. Fuelled by this insight, he worked towards common welfare, religious tolerance, and ethical conduct within the society. Ashoka's commitment even extended to environmental conservation, laying foundations for a just and harmonious society.

His story definitely stands as a timeless reminder that human greatness lies in the delicate art of balancing the elements of life for the well-being of all.

Most of us have grown up with much skewed definition of success. Most of the success stories in media today touch upon one single aspect of our lives. We love rags to riches stories, 90 kgs to 50 kgs weight loss stories, underprivileged to highly educated stories, Alexander the great stories so on and so forth. Is our life that simple? Do any of these things alone ensure more joy or peace that too on consistent basis? Leaving you with this thought to question yourself. Let me answer what it means to designing life here and why?

As per my observation, there are primarily two ways of living –One is when life keeps happening to us and we simply react to life events for having no clue, no knowledge about ourselves– Unconscious living.

Another one is we totally surrender to what happens so there is pure acceptance irrespective of what happens – Ideal State.

The third one and something that I believe in is consciously co-creating our life story till the time we reach the higher stage of total surrender and acceptance. This is a kind of a middle path for seekers like me who have some curiosity towards life and the science of creation but have a long way to attain complete knowledge.

As they say, 'the destination of the train is fixed but how the journey will be is in the hands of the passengers. In this middle path, we consciously decide how to live through this life journey. We make conscious attempt to choose wisely to bring more balance in life.

This path requires active participation in life. This needs looking at all aspects of our human life and bringing balance in every part of our being without neglecting anyone aspect be it Physical (Health), Mental, Emotional, Financial, Professional (Career), Social, Intellectual, Character, Love & Relationships, Parenting, or Spiritual.

Nothing can be overlooked though yes sometimes some aspect of our life takes precedence over the other depending on which stage of life we are in or what challenges we have at any point in time but that's something temporary.

Over long periods, we need to give importance to every area of our lives for better balance. It's essential to periodically assess how we're allocating our time and energy and make adjustments as needed to ensure that no one area dominates our lives at the expense of others.

Striving for balance can lead to greater satisfaction, fulfilment, and overall happiness. If I have missed out something, you are free to add the areas which you think could be part of this.

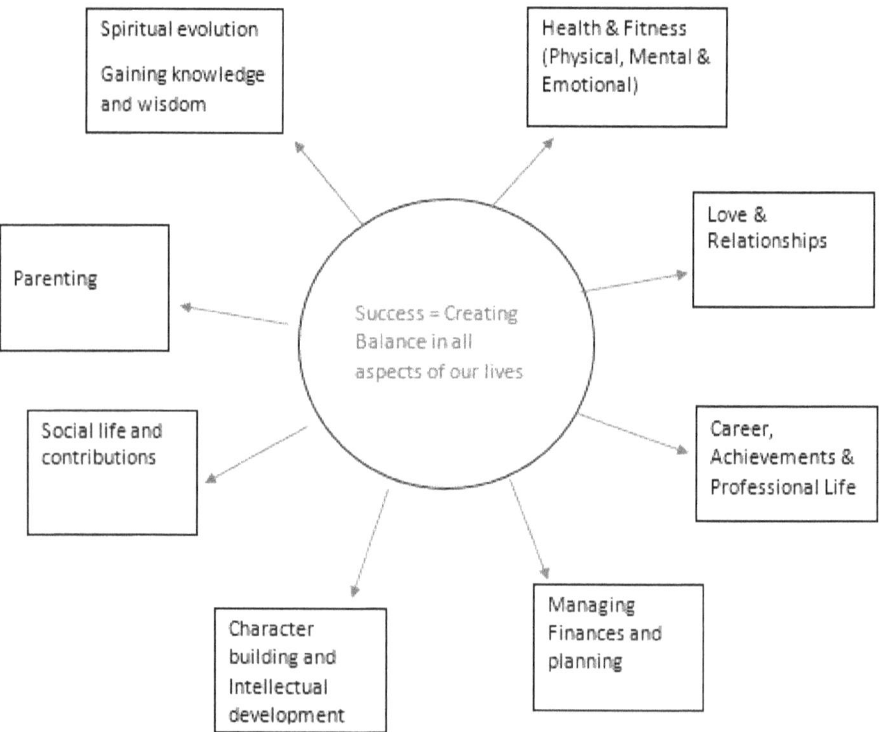

Imagine if you were to write your own story. What is that you would like to see in yourself and what is it that you would like to develop? What would be the theme of your life and what kind of identity you would like to create for yourself in your own mind? Your story means your story. Paradox of life is we all want attention and then we try to fit in by copying what others do.

In this whole exercise its important that your goals and your actions align with your value system and what you truly desire within your heart.

Say in your story, you want to be healthy and loving. What will it take to become that on everyday basis? Let's see a step-by-step approach to creating our own stories.

To start with create an overall vision for your life in your dairy–

The way we have company's mission and vision statement. Similarly write how you would like to see yourself in your story by keeping your likes, your strengths, what motivates you, what inspires you and most importantly what are your values in mind. First page of the dairy you can dedicate to write about yourself initially – your likes, interests, values, inspirations, motivations, strengths etc.

For example - If love and freedom are the most important values to me, my vision statement has to be such that these two become the basis of every choice I make. If these values are compromised, then it would be like anyone else's statement wanting health, happiness and wealth etc.

Since all of us are unique, it's important to understand what matters the most to us while writing our life's vision. Hence do keep your values in mind writing your life's vision or story.

Once you do that, if you wish to go into details, you can further break it down to various levels as our priorities keep changing with age and time.

10 years down the line, 20 years down the line, 30 years down the line, 40 years down the line and 50 years down the line.

Assume, your overall life vision has four important words in it- love, freedom, abundance and spiritual growth.

Now we look at different areas of our lives and make conscious choices to support our overall vision. In each area there are three things to be written

- **Goal statement**
- **Breakdown the goal into results that you want to achieve**
- **Action points – Daily, Weekly/Monthly and Yearly**

Please note: While we are looking at life from all angles and trying to make choices (actions points) based on what we would like to see and attract in our lives, we still would need to leave the final outcome on to the universe. We still don't have the complete picture of why we have to go through what we go through at times. Choices are in our hands, results are not.

Most importantly while working on the plan, when it comes to short-term vs long-term and easy vs difficult, please do not ignore the long-term consequences even if it means difficult choices or actions in the present.

Coming back to understanding how to work on every aspect. Let's see with examples in each case.

1. Health& Fitness

This comes first and above everything. Here's an example

Goal statement: I have perfect health, shape, weight and I look younger with every passing day. I have lots of energy and enthusiasm. I am emotionally well balanced.

Results to achieve based on person's condition

- Weight- 52 kgs approx.
- Sugar and triglycerides below 100 mg/dl

- Hb1AC- Below 5.9%
- Muscle strength
- Efficient metabolism
- Flat belly
- Glowing Skin, Healthy hair to look young
- Gum health and smiling face so on and so forth
- Anger, anxiety and fear Control

Action points

Daily: Drinking smoothie or ABC or any detox juice every day first thing in the morning. Eating nutritious food. Stop junk during binge watching. Sleeping on time. Dinner 3 hrs before sleeping. Reducing sugar intake. Reducing screen time, daily meditation, morning rituals (starting your day well), hot and cold water therapy during shower, Face yoga for skin and applying natural oil/cream at night etc depending on what works for you and what have you learnt otherwise seek information.

Weekly: 3 days a week Gym for strength training, 2 days a week yoga. Salt water bath, hair oiling and spa. Hypnotherapy sessions for anger and fear.

Monthly: Twice a month, hiking, trekking or jungle walk. Pre-planning the dates and calendar accordingly every month.

Yearly: One trek or hike or attending a meditation retreat. Taking anger management course to learn and manage emotions.

You can create your own timetable to plan the day which supports your health. Why wait for sad and bad medical reports as wake up call. This is just an example. **Your story is your choice based on what you value the most, what your goals are and what you would like to see as results then decide your own actions points and start working.**

2. Love and Relationships

This has to come in the second place because as per research our sense of well-being (Happy feeling) depends a lot of our relationships with ourselves, with our family and the society. People, who have good friends and supportive families, live longer. But here too, we need to choose our part first. What we need to do instead of what others have to do for us.

Let's look at relationships in circles for **a married adult.** This is not based on the importance but on the level of involvement basis needs and participation.

The first is the relationship with ourselves. So we are the centre of the circle.

Then is the relationship with our spouse. The innermost circle.

Then is the relationship with our children. The next circle.

Then is the relationship with our parents. The next circle.

Then is the relationship with our siblings.

Then comes the extended family. And then comes the society which includes our professional relationships as well. For many of us our friends circle, our colleagues may form part of our innermost circle. That's perfectly fine. Your life is your choice.

Thing to remember are relationships that form the basis of our being. In fact, most of our difficult life lessons come out of our relationships because the more baggage we come with, the more imbalance we create within and in our environment either by doing things not required at all or by not doing things which are truly required.

Besides, having strong likes and strong dislikes is a recipe for failure especially when it comes to relationships. School of life always catches our weakness.

Let's see how to work on this aspect using an example

Goal Statement: My life is filled with love and all of my relationships are harmonious and peaceful.

Results to achieve for the above goal

- Self-love
- Blossoming romance and love in married life
- Happy upbringing of children, giving them required support, being the right example and directing them in the right direction- Doing our part right

- Taking care of old parents, helping them in need and most importantly ensuring that they feel loved and respected.
- Grow healthy relationship and bonds with siblings
- Ensuring healthy connections with extended family, cousins etc
- Creating a positive impact at work and in society at large with our behaviour, love and care. Being sensitive towards others – from people on road to the animals in the jungle to help at home.

Actions Points

- 'Loving oneself' comes with 'improving oneself' caveat. They are not independent of each other. Most of us have misinterpreted self-help books and therapies to continue to remain in our respective comfort zones.
- When we start loving our self, we start taking care of our physical, mental and emotional well-being. How can a person who loves himself do his own harm? Loving oneself comes with lot of actions that support our life. From accepting failures and unfairness to focusing on what feels good to the company you choose to keep… everything shows ones love towards oneself.
- Date nights with the spouse once every week. Travelling just with the spouse once every quarter for holidaying. Choosing a common activity or interest or joining a hobby class together.
- Calling parents every week just to listen. Getting their full check-up done once a year. Sending cake, gifts on all important occasions. Spending time with them on occasions. Taking them out etc.
- Meeting siblings once every quarter at least depending on the distance. Calling siblings once a week at least. Planning vacations/ holidays with siblings.

- Calling and wishing all elderly relatives on important occasions. Arranging/planning extended family get-togethers once a year to start with. Get together with all friends once in six months at least.
- Being calm on road so it's important to listen to calming music while driving. No shouting on anyone on the road no matter what.
- Giving new clothes and financial help to house helps at least once a year.

These are just some examples. The goal is yours. The action points too have to be yours. No of times to do something, what to do and how to do is also totally your choice depending on what works for you.

Point to note: Peaceful relationships and fulfilling the duties go hand in hand. Peace is the natural result of how we live and act in our lives. No one can give this to someone else or take this from the other. However, 'Don't bother' is a state that all irresponsible & all imbalanced call as peace.

3. Career& Achievements

Most of us find it easy to put goals here as career becomes a priority from school itself. In fact, we are brought up with the idea of success based on career and professional achievements. Yes, this is very important but it's only one aspect of our lives.

To manage risks, it is advisable not to put all eggs in one basket and so putting all energies just in one area of life may lead to disappointments because at the end of every achievement, one would face the question of 'now what'. It's an endless chase. Balancing career and professional achievements with other joys of life usually gives more satisfaction during the journey. Let's learn with an example

Goal Statement: To run x dollars venture by the year 2025 and win x award have x balance in the account by the year 2030, creating x no of jobs by 2028 or

Promotion as x(designation) by the mid-2024, while working on x projects among x (kind of people), winning x award, becoming a public speaker and sharing the ideas.

Could be anything that you want from your career.

Results to achieve

- Developing the idea and Securing Investment
- Developing a great team
- Achieving X targets consistently and managing great relations with the boss and the team for promotion. So on and so forth

What to achieve (exact numbers) by when to achieve are important to have clarity in our own minds. Action points will help break down the big goal into smaller actions to be taken consistently.

Action points

- Preparing a vision board by this month end to clearly mention all that I wish to achieve and by when
- Taking courses and listening to A, B, C
- Hiring 5 smart people for the team for existing roles
- Find mentors for professional life to guide by this month end.
- Meeting x no of suppliers/ customers every month
- Having discussion on your professional growth path with the boss in next two days which you have been avoiding for a month now.

4. Managing Finances &Planning

No matter how much one earns budgeting and planning depending on various personal goals is important just the way any company or a corporate structure does it.

In the smallest of the company to the biggest one with huge cash reserves, finances and planning is necessarily done however in our personal lives, so many of us ignore this or don't do financial planning in details. With very low income, people think there is no point having any goal and with huge incomes, people don't keep a track of the details out of sheer careless attitude. Result - no clarity.

Not just earning but managing money or finances too plays a very important role in our well-being because money is an answer to freedom in many areas of our lives. Financial stability provides freedom and flexibility. It allows individuals to make choices without being constrained by financial limitations. And mishandling of finances can even create marital discord.

Here's a sample to explain how to plan. Your goals could be completely different of course and would depend on your age and priorities at that age.

Goal Statement: I am able to fulfil all my duties from building home to creating assets to child's education and marriage comfortably and retire at the age of 55. I also want to create healthy family bonds by way of taking family vacations twice in a year.

Results to achieve

- Children's education & marriage –Estimated corpus – 2crores in next 15 years
- Retirement Corpus to retire at the age of 55 yrs comfortably– 5 crores, in next 20 years

- Home loan corpus- 3 crores, in next 10 years
- Yearly travel budget- 10 lacs

Actions points

- Monthly budgeting – Tracking expenses and income either on Excel sheet or personal finance apps.
- Monthly/Weekly regular savings – Using retirement calculator, put all financial goals and then calculate the corpus needed and then the monthly savings amount to be saved. Creating regular savings plan for X amount per month on basis of the calculations.
- Action point could also be to start with Opening FD accounts or Mutual funds accounts or share trading a/c.
- Investment Portfolio – Divide investment into Debt, Equity, Real Estate, FDs, Gold and bonds.
- Passive income generation - Looking at other avenues to generate income. Learning to trade for example or starting your own coaching.

5. Character building and Intellectual development

One of the last priorities when it comes to the definition of success in the present times but this is the base on which the path to success is built. This ideally should come first.

Self-discipline, perseverance, keeping the word and not giving up easily are very much part of character building if one wants professional and personal success.

I have always felt that the more challenging career choices we make, the more is the grind and test of the character be it in a job or entrepreneurship. Ability to go past failures, learn and go on are needed to build character.

However, almost everywhere the news heading is about the net worth generated by someone but there is hardly any mention of the specific character qualities that paved the way to success. Character is the result of daily habits; habits result from the behaviours and the behaviours come out of the thoughts & beliefs (our value system)

Let's see an example

Goals (say of a teenager): Handling all life situations calmly and patiently. Working with laser sharp focus.

Results to achieve

- Anger Management
- Focus in studies and sports

Actions Points

- Learning Anger Management. Deep breaths or counting when facing a situation one doesn't like.
- Taking up a course to learn anger management.
- Finding a mentor.
- Changing friends circle to ensure good environment. Developing focus by doing one thing at a time.
- Not watch TV while eating or no loud music while sleeping or studying from today.
- Doing daily meditation - 6am to 6.30 am. Removing all distractions from the study table this weekend. Cleaning and de-cluttering the room on Sunday.

6. Social Life & Contributions

Our thoughts, actions, feelings, emotions, everything travels, everything has an impact, a reaction. Given that we are social and keep interacting with others and the environment, the effect is much more. Impact can be good or bad, active or passive depending on what we choose. For our own expansion, the more active and the more positive impact we make outside of us, the better return would come back as a reaction of our action.

Imagine if no one ever thought of curing diseases. Imagine if no one ever thought of inventing the bulb. Imagine if no one ever thought of saving our natural resources, forests and animals.

Whatever we have today is because someone decided to think beyond his/her needs, because someone decided to contribute for the betterment of the society. There are numerous ways to contribute from teaching to creating to helping people physically in difficult situations and more. What one can do is one's choice and capability. However, it is vital to have concrete goals here too. One can of course start small but a contribution is very much part of human success. Let's assume an example for understanding.

Goal: Impact 1000 student lives with my maths teaching skills. Contribute towards causes like – child education and wildlife.

Results to achieve

- 1000 students would mean 100 in a year to reach 1000 in next 10 years.
- 20-30 offline and remaining online using Youtube
- Weekend teaching in the apartment for all under privileged kids.

Action Points

- Join weekend teaching program
- Talk to NGOs- prepare the list first
- Start teaching the kids of all security guards and maids who work in the apartment so on and so forth.

7. Spiritual Aspect

It's not the question of being spiritual or being material and worldly given that there are various levels. It's simply a necessity to be more conscious of every action and mindful of every response to the event/situation we may or may not like. Mindfulness helps us regulate our emotions, allowing us to respond more calmly and rationally to challenging situations. Instead of reacting impulsively out of frustration or anger, we can decide and choose how to respond thoughtfully.

From my personal experience, this is a basic need. Sanity is a basic need not just for oneself but for everyone around. Sanity comes from being conscious of our response. Being conscious of our responses is a cornerstone of maintaining mental and emotional balance.

But yes, despite everyday practice, I fail. Not just once or twice but many times and it feels like going back to zero every time. But then I think... what am I failing at? Controlling mind and its reactions? That anyway is a long journey. We pass at one lesson, something else comes up, and something harder comes up. There is no befooling here; life is a deep cleaning process. Unless even the slightest ounce of dirt remains, we will keep failing and falling during tests.

Having perfect actions and reactions is a long journey. Who knows I could have been worse. So, I am still at it. I haven't perfected the art but if out of 10 times, even 5 times I am acting properly, that's a progress and that is due to my work on my mind and body.

Let's see this with an example on how to develop this aspect. I have been saying that your goals, the results you want to achieve and your action points are completely your choice. This is just an example.

Goal: Being more peaceful. Have fewer reactions. Develop focus and be centred in all sorts of situations.

Results to achieve

- Peaceful sleep
- Clarity in thinking
- Reading 5 spiritual books a year
- Take 1 wellness retreat a year
- Finish 1 week meditation course by this month end

Actions points

- Meditate everyday for at least 10 min to start with and increase overtime
- Start with one mantra and one small puja everyday before leaving for work.
- Journaling to express myself, release what I need to and write my experiences.
- Training the mind and body both by going for a trek within next 3 months.
- Changing the circle of friends and food habits.
- Sleeping by 10 pm and having 7-8 hrs of sleep.
- Book and plan the wellness retreat.
- Read 10-20 pages each day so on and so forth.

8. Parenting

In the previous generation, most of the parenting challenges centered around money and being able to provide for children and family. Not getting everything easily brought the sense of self discipline among children as they decided to work towards creating better life stories than their parents.

But in this generation, when children have over exposure to everything, the parenting challenges especially for middle class and above are not about giving but about not giving or controlling what's not needed and could be potentially harmful for kids.

So, now that we have *roti kapda makaan*, most life lessons come from relationships and parenting.

While we can think that parenting comes naturally to us as soon as we give birth to a child, it doesn't seem so. It may be true for other animals but to rear a highly emotional and intelligent human being ensuring mere survival is not all, given that most human stories across the world have childhood issues as the cause of pain. And hence parenting success has to be part of our overall success story.

We definitely need to have goals to keep upgrading our parenting skills so as to be able to manoeuvre when faced with different parenting challenges that crop up as times change.

Goal: To be patient, kind yet assertive with my child.

Results to achieve

- Now allowing phone and Wi- Fi after 10 pm at home
- Developing connection and deep bond with my child

Action Points

- Play with my child two to three times a week especially over weekends
- Eating at least one meal together as a family without any screen
- Working on self by moving from reactions to actions.
- Take help of therapists, there are always some cases beyond our capacity and knowledge to solve. So on and so forth.

As mentioned before, feel free to include additional facets into this list that align closely with your life. The objective is to adopt a holistic approach towards creating a successful life, focusing on personal growth and making progress consistently, even through small incremental steps.

All the very best on your journey to designing your best self. Stay Balanced and Blessed!

ADDITIONAL READING AND REFERENCES

Food Chart

We all need some essential nutrients that must come from our food; they are vital for disease prevention, growth, and good health. Primarily there are two categories: macronutrients and micronutrients.

Macronutrients are eaten in large amounts and include the primary building blocks of your diet — protein, carbohydrates, and fat — which provide your body with energy. Vitamins and minerals are micronutrients, and small doses go a long way. There are six main groups of essential micronutrients and macronutrients.

Carbohydrates: Carbohydrates are the sugars, starches and fibres present in the products of fruits, grains, vegetables and milk. They are the primary source of energy for the body.

They are of two types- Simple and Complex. Simple carbohydrates are present in such foods as table sugar and syrups. Complex carbohydrates contain longer sugar molecular chains than mere carbohydrates. Since complex carbohydrates have longer chains, they take longer than simple carbohydrates to break down and provide more lasting energy in the body.

Now you can guess who needs immediate sugar rush (simple carbs) and who needs slow release of sugars (complex carbs). With age and less body movement, we need slow release of sugars hence more complex carbohydrates.

Proteins: Proteins are the building blocks of living beings. Protein is present in every human cell. An amino acid chain forms the basic building block of proteins. For our body to repair damaged cells and create new ones, we need protein in our daily diet. Functions of protein include storage, hormone signalling, transport, muscle contraction and digestive enzyme. The ability to digest the proteins is very important before anyone starts mindless protein intake for body building.

Vitamins: The vitamins are natural and essential nutrients, required in small quantities and play a major role in growth and development, repair and healing wounds, maintaining healthy bones and tissues, for the proper functioning of an immune system, and other biological functions. There are thirteen different types of vitamins and all are required for the metabolic processes.

Vitamins are either fat soluble or water soluble. Vitamin A, D, E and K are fat-soluble vitamins, need fat to be absorbed in the system. Vitamin B and C are water-soluble vitamins. Water-soluble vitamins are not stored in our body as its excess gets excrete through the urine. Therefore, these vitamins need to be replenished constantly.

Minerals: They are inorganic substances required by the human body to function correctly. There are many examples of minerals in food; these include: Calcium, Phosphorus, Potassium, Sodium, Iodine, Iron, Magnesium

The body also requires other minerals in trace amounts such as selenium, cobalt and molybdenum. These elements are known to have a specific function in the human body.

Fats: According to nutrition facts, fats are an essential part of the diet and play an important role in maintaining a healthy life. Fat happens to be the most concentrated source of energy in the diet, belong to a group of elements called lipids, and they are all combinations of saturated and unsaturated fats. Fats play a major role in controlling inflammation, blood coagulation, and brain development. It also serves as a storage unit for storing the body's extra calories in fat cells or adipose tissue that helps to insulate the body. There are four types- Saturated Fats, Monosaturated Fats, Trans Fats and Poly Saturated Fats.

Saturated Fat is responsible for bad cholesterol. They are found in most animal products like cheese, milk, meat and so on and hence one must limit the quantity of intake.

Monounsaturated fats are healthy fats found in Avocados, Macadamia nuts, Peanuts, Olives and Olive oil. It plays a vital role in protecting the heart and is also involved in supporting insulin sensitivity, fat storage, weight loss, and healthy energy levels.

Polyunsaturated fats are healthy fats, which are abundantly found in both plant and animal foods, such as vegetable oils, Walnuts, Flax seeds, salmon, etc. These fats include both Omega 3 and Omega 6 fats. Omega 3 helps reduce inflammation and supports healthy hormone levels and cell membranes. Omega 6 fatty acids play an important role in supporting healthy brain and muscle functioning

Trans fats are also called unsaturated fatty acids or trans fatty acids. These fats are naturally obtained in several foods such as beef, lamb, whole milk, cheese, cream, and butter from cattle. Trans fats are present in many processed foods as a result of hydrogenation.

Here's is a food chart to understand which food contains what. Please note: Not just the amount of carbohydrates, protein, fat or fibre is important but also their nature. Some are easily digestible while some are not. Some have better effect on the body while the other may not have. Hence, it is not enough to know the just the calorie count or amount of the macro nutrient in the specific food to decide on your diet. Do consult a nutritionist if required.

Protein Antibody, Enzymes, Messenger, Structural, Transport and Storage. Below is protein value per 100 gm of the food	Vitamins- A, B1, B2, B3, B5, B6, B9, B12, C, D, E, K, Beta Carotene, and Lycopene are 14 essential nutrients	Minerals-Calcium, Phosphorus, Potassium, Sodium, Iodine, Iron, Magnesium
Soyabean 52g	Fish 9 out of 14 nutrients A, B1, B2, B3, B5, B6, B12, D, and E	Calcium: Almonds, Carrots, Milk, Broccoli, Canned Fish, Papaya, Garlic, and Cashew
Amaranth 14g	Dark leafy vegetables A, B2, B3, B6, B9, C, E, K, and Beta-Carotene	Chloride: Table Salt, Soy Sauce, liver Unprocessed Meat, Milk and Peanuts
Quinoa 14g	Seeds 6 of 14, B1, B2, B3, B5, B5, B6, and E.	Copper: Crab, Lobster, Mussels, Oysters, Nuts, Wholegrains and Yeast extract

Protein Antibody, Enzymes, Messenger, Structural, Transport and Storage. Below is protein value per 100 gm of the food	**Vitamins- A, B1, B2, B3, B5, B6, B9, B12, C, D, E, K, Beta Carotene, and Lycopene are 14 essential nutrients**	**Minerals-Calcium, Phosphorus, Potassium, Sodium, Iodine, Iron, Magnesium**
Millet 11g	Broccoli is a good source for 6 of 14 A, B9, C, E, K, and Beta Carotene.	Iodine: Seafood, Seaweed and Iodised salt
Buckwheat 13.2 g	Pork is a good source for 6 of 14 essential vitamins. B1, B2, B3, B5, B6, and D.	Iron: Meat, Eggs, Beans, Baked Potato, Dried Fruits, Green Leafy Vegetables, Whole and Enriched Grains
White/brown sugar 7.9g	Beef and lamb is a good source for 5 of 14 essential vitamins. These include Vitamins B2, B3, B5, B6, and B9.	Magnesium: Honey, Almonds, Seafood, Tuna, Chocolates, Pineapple, Pecans, Artichokes, and Green Leafy Vegetables

(Contd.)

Protein Antibody, Enzymes, Messenger, Structural, Transport and Storage. Below is protein value per 100 gm of the food	**Vitamins- A, B1, B2, B3, B5, B6, B9, B12, C, D, E, K, Beta Carotene, and Lycopene are 14 essential nutrients**	**Minerals-Calcium, Phosphorus, Potassium, Sodium, Iodine, Iron, Magnesium**
Wild rice 4g	Mushrooms are a good source for 4 of 14 essential vitamins. These include Vitamins B2, B3, B5, and D.	Manganese: Cereals, Nuts, Oils, Vegetables and Wholegrains
Couscous 13.6g	Nuts are a good source for 4 of 14 essential vitamins. These include Vitamins B1, B2, B6, and E.	Sodium: Table Salt, Cheese, Milk, Soy Sauce, and Unprocessed Meat
Wheat 11.8g	Eggs are a good source for 4 of 14 essential vitamins. These include Vitamins B2, B5, B12, and D.	Sulphur: Cheese, Eggs, Nuts, Turnips, Onions, Fish, Wheat Germ, Cucumbers, Corn, Cauliflower, and Broccoli

Protein Antibody, Enzymes, Messenger, Structural, Transport and Storage. Below is protein value per 100 gm of the food	**Vitamins- A, B1, B2, B3, B5, B6, B9, B12, C, D, E, K, Beta Carotene, and Lycopene are 14 essential nutrients**	**Minerals-Calcium, Phosphorus, Potassium, Sodium, Iodine, Iron, Magnesium**
Ragi7.3g	Bell Peppers are a good source for 4 of 14 essential vitamins. A, and C, Beta-Carotene, and Lycopene	Phosphorus: Mushrooms, Meat, Cashews, Oats, Fish, Beans, Squash, Pecans, Carrots, and Almonds
Jowar 10.4g	Avocados are a good source for 4 of 14 essential vitamins. B5, B6, B9, and E.	Potassium: Spinach, Apples, Oranges, Tomatoes, Papaya, Bananas, Lemons, Celery, Mushrooms, Pecans, Raisins, Pineapple, Rice, Cucumbers, Strawberries, Figs, Brussels Sprouts, and Legume

(Contd.)

Protein Antibody, Enzymes, Messenger, Structural, Transport and Storage. Below is protein value per 100 gm of the food	**Vitamins- A, B1, B2, B3, B5, B6, B9, B12, C, D, E, K, Beta Carotene, and Lycopene are 14 essential nutrients**	**Minerals-Calcium, Phosphorus, Potassium, Sodium, Iodine, Iron, Magnesium**
Oats-13.6g	Peas are a good source for 4 of 14 essential vitamins. A, B1, E, and Beta Carotene.	Zinc: Beef, Pork, Dark Meat, Chicken, Cashews, Almonds, Peanuts, Beans, Split Peas, and Lentil
Kidney beans 22.6g	Butternut Squash is a good source for 4 of 14 essential vitamins. These include Vitamins A, B1, E, and Beta Carotene.	
Chickpeas 19g	Tropical Fruits a good source for 4 of 14 essential vitamins. These include Vitamins A, B1, E, and Lycopene	

Protein Antibody, Enzymes, Messenger, Structural, Transport and Storage. Below is protein value per 100 gm of the food	**Vitamins- A, B1, B2, B3, B5, B6, B9, B12, C, D, E, K, Beta Carotene, and Lycopene are 14 essential nutrients**	**Minerals-Calcium, Phosphorus, Potassium, Sodium, Iodine, Iron, Magnesium**
Blackbeans 21g	Dried Fruits are a good source for 4 of 14 essential vitamins. These include Vitamins A, B6, K, and Beta Carotene	
Mungbeans 24g	Asparagus High in Vitamins B1, B9, K, and Lycopene	
Green lentils 17.9g	**Carrots** High in Vitamin A, Beta Carotene, and Lycopene	
Red lentil 7g	Lentils High in Vitamin B9	
Milk 3.3 g	**Sweet Potatoes** High in Vitamins A, B5, and Beta Carotene	
Paneer 18.3 g	**Beans** High in Vitamins B1, and B9	

(Contd.)

Protein Antibody, Enzymes, Messenger, Structural, Transport and Storage. Below is protein value per 100 gm of the food	Vitamins- A, B1, B2, B3, B5, B6, B9, B12, C, D, E, K, Beta Carotene, and Lycopene are 14 essential nutrients	Minerals-Calcium, Phosphorus, Potassium, Sodium, Iodine, Iron, Magnesium
Cheese 24.1g	**Cheese** High in Vitamins B2, B5, and B12	
Yogurt 3.1g	**Tomatoes & Guava** High in Vitamin C, and Lycopene	
Cream 2g	**Bananas** High in Vitamin B6	
Almonds 18.4g	Citurs Fruits and Berries High in Vitamin C	
Peanuts 25.8g	**Peanuts** High in Vitamin B3	
Cashew 21.2g	**Plant Oils (Olive Oil)** High in Vitamins E and K	
Pista 19.8g	**Kiwifruit** High in Vitamins C and E	

Protein Antibody, Enzymes, Messenger, Structural, Transport and Storage. Below is protein value per 100 gm of the food	**Vitamins- A, B1, B2, B3, B5, B6, B9, B12, C, D, E, K, Beta Carotene, and Lycopene are 14 essential nutrients**	**Minerals-Calcium, Phosphorus, Potassium, Sodium, Iodine, Iron, Magnesium**
Soy nuts 39.5g	**Dry Roasted Soybeans** High in Vitamin B1	
Chestnuts 3.4g	**Shellfish** High in Vitamins B2, B12, and E	
Hazelnuts 15g		
Pine nuts 13.9g		
Walnuts15.6g		
Pecan nuts 9.2g		
Sunflower seeds 21g		
Pumpkin seeds 19g		
Chia seeds 17g		
Flax seeds 18g		
Hemp seeds 30g		
Sesame seeds 18g		
Poppy seeds 18g		
Amaranth seeds		
Eggs 13.3 g		
Soy milk 3.3g		
Tofu 8.1 g		
Salmon 20.5g		

(Contd.)

Protein Antibody, Enzymes, Messenger, Structural, Transport and Storage. Below is protein value per 100 gm of the food	Vitamins- A, B1, B2, B3, B5, B6, B9, B12, C, D, E, K, Beta Carotene, and Lycopene are 14 essential nutrients	Minerals-Calcium, Phosphorus, Potassium, Sodium, Iodine, Iron, Magnesium
Tuna 29g		
Mackerel 19g		
Lobster 20.5g		
Crab 17.4g		
Pomfret 17g		
Chicken 25.9g		
Lamb 20.6g		
Beef 22.6g		
Mutton 18.5g		

www.ingramcontent.com/pod-product-compliance
Lightning Source LLC
LaVergne TN
LVHW021152160826
845679LV00024B/2096

9798892775762